SO YOU WANT TO R

C000175667

ULTR

How to prepare for ultimate endurance

SO YOU WANT TO RUN AN
ULTRA
How to prepare for ultimate endurance

Andy Mouncey

CROWOOD

First published in 2014 by
The Crowood Press Ltd
Ramsbury, Marlborough
Wiltshire SN8 2HR

www.crowood.com

Dedication
For the pupils, staff and parents of these schools who came with me on my 'Cracking The Spine Race' project
in the winter of 2013–14:

Edale Primary School
Horton-in-Ribblesdale Primary School
Cowling Primary School
Caton Primary School
Grassington Primary School
Grindleford Primary School
Bamford Primary School
Kirkby Malham Primary School
Bradwell Junior School
Riverside Junior School
Hope Valley College
Settle College
Seaham School of Technology

British Library Cataloguing-in-Publication Data
A catalogue record for this book is available from the British Library.

ISBN 978 1 84797 830 1

Graphic design and layout by Peggy Issenman, www.peggyandco.ca
Printed and bound in India by Replika Press Pvt Ltd

Contents

About the Author

In 1983 a seven-teen-year-old Andy Mouncey started his first training diary in order to record the results of his first race: a ninety-minute out-ing over the half-mar-athon distance in Ilkley, West Yorkshire, UK. He has been writing and racing ever since then, starting on the fells of the north of England as a teenager before progressing to triathlon. He signed off seventeen years in that sport by set-ting new fastest stage times for the Enduroman Arch To Arc Challenge in 2003: a 300-mile solo triathlon linking London and Paris via an English Channel swim.

Since 2004 he hasn't swum a stroke in anger, concentrating instead on trail ultra running. He has finished the Lakeland 100 – the UK's most prestigious trail one-hundred miler – three times, being placed second twice.

He is an accredited athletics coach, personal trainer and conditioning coach who has been coaching, training and mentoring clients from sport, business and education since 2000. He is also an inspirational award-winning pro-fessional speaker and a previously published author who has appeared on radio and TV.

In 2013 he designed and launched a ground-breaking learning programme for school pupils based around an ultra-running challenge linked to his own attempt to finish The Spine Race in January 2014 – the UK's most brutal winter ultra covering the 268 miles of the Pennine Way national trail. *Cracking The Spine* reached 1,600 pupils across thirteen schools, raised thousands of pounds for the charity Sport Relief, and is very much a project in progress.

He is married and lives with his family in the north of England.

www.bigandscaryrunning.com

Other books by Andy:
London To Paris The Hard Way
Magic, Madness and Ultramarathon Running

CHAPTER 1

An Introduction To Ultra Running

Can Anyone Run Ultras?

'*So, Andy, do you think anyone can run ultras?*'

Such was the final question from my audience at the 2013 Keswick Mountain Festival in the English Lake District. Little did I know that at least one person in the audience was willing me to give a positive response …

Welcome to our world.

'Well …' Cue big pause while gathering thoughts, 'we already know *It's Not About The Distance*, don't we?'

Nods and knowing grins from lovely onside and on-message audience.

'The distance just brings the challenge of *compound* and *cumulative*, remember? That's more stuff to deal with more often and for longer. As long as we're sufficiently motivated it's gonna be about the other stuff: keeping your contact points intact, (cue overly dramatic elevation of right foot into audience sight-line) 'controlling your pace – especially in the first third of a race – and managing your mood. The good news is that those are all skills that can be taught.'

More knowing grins and nods are sent my way.

'I reckon it's only a matter of time before someone makes a reality TV documentary with just this in mind. Look at the precidents – actor David Walliams swimming the English Channel to raise money for the charity Comic Relief a few years ago – OK it isn't running, but it is ultra distance and while he was a good swimmer to start with, that was still a huge ask. Likewise comedian Eddie Izzard and his forty-odd marathons in around the same number of days, and comedian John Bishop doing his Paris to London triathlon thing for Sport Relief last year. Now Comic Relief is back next year: anyone want to lay any odds?'

Pause for dramatic effect.

'So as long as the basic unit and body systems are functioning, my answer to the question is yes, I do. Absolutely.'

REVELATIONS FROM REAL RUNNERS

How I Got Started and Why I Do It

Paul Parrish

On 22 November 2000 I walked into an office of the company where I worked and asked for one of the London Marathon charity places that they had set aside for staff. They wanted to know who it was for, and when I said it was for me, they laughed and refused to hand it over. 'It will be a waste,' they told me, 'you'll never do it!'

The reason for their scepticism was that I was a thirty-five-year-old man who weighed 15½ stone and chain smoked cigars (three packets a day). I drank every lunchtime and every evening. I smelt of booze permanently, and would feel light-headed going up stairs. I couldn't use the London tube because I would sweat so much I would arrive at destinations cloaked in embarrassment and shame. An active alcoholic, I lived in a world of shame and guilt.

I finally persuaded them to give me that marathon place, and in the following April I crossed the finishing line sobbing tears of joy. I had begun to run and I have never stopped, and I continue to run to put as much distance as I can between the man that was and the man that is here now.

Addiction is a shocking half-life of existence, but learning to counter it has given me crucial tools to allow me to take on ultra distance running. I have learnt that an addict has incredible willpower. I thought I was spineless and weak willed, until another addict pointed out that it takes amazing willpower to have a drink at 11am when your body is wrecked from the previous night. I now know that no matter how long the run, or how difficult the terrain, I have the willpower to keep going. Nothing is as hard as having that drink when your body is physically screaming at you to stop!

I have learnt never to look at a run in its entirety, but to chop it up into segments and take each piece as it comes. Sure, have a strategy, but be prepared to adapt and adjust. An addict is told to live each day one day at a time. It is no good look at an entire life without your drug of choice – the addict couldn't handle it. Instead just adapt to each day and take that. The days soon become years, just as each mile of a run soon becomes an entire race.

Finally, ultra running has made me understand privilege: the beauty of the countryside that I run across, the power of a beautiful sunrise and the luxury of a body that keeps running and feels strong. I could never have imagined that this could be my life. As I run the long miles that we ultra runners have to cover, there is never a moment when I don't count my blessings. No matter why you run, please remember how privileged we are to be able to do this.

Sharon McDonald

FREEDOM! The
freedom from
normal life. If we
are lucky, we all
find in life's journey
something that
makes us feel so
high that the hardest

thing is putting it into words. The complete
freedom of putting one foot in front of the
other, and the excitement of what's around the
next corner or over the next brow is what does
it for me – running is so simple. The ultra runs
give me the opportunity to have that feeling for
so much longer – not that I'm greedy – but the
ultimate satisfaction of having trained hard,
enjoyed and finished a race is like no other:
honest!

The Fellsman race on 15 May 2011 became
my intro into ultra running, the training of
not just the body but also the mind. It also
became my first benchmark. At 62 miles and
11,000ft, covering some of the best scenery in
the Yorkshire Dales, it was a good place to start
– and it being on my doorstep also helped. I
soon realized I enjoyed the training no matter
how hard or how long, and having an ultimate
aim made it exciting, especially as I could see
and feel the difference the training was making.
The result was 14.04 hours, and yes it was
painful, yes it was the hardest physical/mental
challenge I had done, but wow!

The *wows* over the next few years have
become bigger and bigger, and my addictive
need for that ultimate feeling of pure freedom has seen me do more and more. The
second benchmark was a five-day continuous
multi-sport adventure race. This is where I
learnt that I really don't need much sleep, just
sheer determination, great team mates, a good
mental attitude, and the ability to always focus
on the next checkpoint.

Alex Mason

It started as an aid
to my kickboxing
fitness, but we
moved, and as there
were no classes
near my house, I
stopped kickboxing
but upped my running. After an injury at
Nottingham Half Marathon I switched to trails
and progressed from there. I'm a late starter
to running, only getting into it in the last five
years.

After much thinking – which ultra running
is very good at helping with – this is the
current rationale: they may not be the correct
answers – but hey, who's marking me!

• Because it's madness! Getting to about
80K in a 100K ultra and at the penultimate
checkpoint asking how much further and I
get 20K! Only 20K! That's a half marathon.
Most people would see doing one as a
massive challenge, but I've just done nearly
four back to back, and have only one more
to go
• It's a challenge. I want to push myself
outside my comfort zone and do something
that just sounds impossible to do. I love
the thrill of the race, to be pushed to the
limits and beyond; it expands your own
boundaries

- Because I love it! I love being out in the open on some wild adventure, running around and exploring new places
- To inspire my two children. We went to the Olympics in 2012 and it was very inspirational, but there was an 'élitist' disconnection between the athletes and reality. I wanted to prove to them that they can do whatever they want to if they put themselves to it: that their Daddy can run 100K in one go! That if their Daddy can do it, then they can too

Am I any different as a result of all this? I don't really think that I am. I was always like this but never did anything about it until now.

Sal Chaffey

Unlike a lot of things in life, with running, what you put in normally equates to what you get back. My biggest challenge was the Lake District Bob Graham Round (65 miles and 27,000ft of ascent, to be completed in under twenty-four hours). As well as the fitness, there's a lot of basic house-keeping aspects of preparation, such as route recce, planning a schedule, maps, food, road support, and support on the route from five pairs of pacers. I use this methodical approach to all races, getting kit ready and starting anti-inflammatories the day before, and recce (or Google Earth) the route.

With any challenge in life, I look back on my Bob Graham Round and think, I did the BG, so I can do this …

I get a lot of satisfaction from looking at where I've run on the map, and am enjoying my GPS tracking app on my phone. In 2012 I did the London to Brighton Race (Extreme Running) and reccied the whole route the month before.

Ultra running is a great way of exploring all these places, and I haven't even run abroad yet! I started blogging about a year ago, and enjoy sharing photos with friends and family as well as reading other people's blogs to find out about potential events.

Rob Shenton

'What are you running away from?' is a common question I got when people found out I ran ultras. It was not until I really started running that I realized there might actually be an issue. When I run I love the solitude, I like going through issues in my mind, I like the peace I encounter – I could lose myself for hours. But I always knew there was something more. It came to light when I finished events. I had achieved such great things, beyond the limits of normal human endurance, and yet I still did not feel complete.

I realized there was something wrong. After a while and with some help, it turned out that for many years I had been battling depression, as do one in four people in the UK. My mind can make me suffer immeasurably before I even consider running. In a way, all the preparation that ultra running takes helps fight that depression because it eliminates doubt and gives me faith in my abilities. But I know that with depression, if the doubt sets in and takes root, it is an incredibly hard thing to shift. So what was I to do?

Running long distances can teach you lessons that can help you in life. Something a friend suggested to me to help eliminate the doubt I could have encountered on the Marathon des Sables has stayed with me. It is a great little exercise and can be a brilliant pick-up for anyone when a low hits. Prior to flying off to the MdS I contacted my closest friends and asked them one simple question: 'Give me three reasons why I will be successful'. They all obliged and emailed me back reasons. I printed them off in small font – weight is everything when carrying it over 250 miles – waterproofed it and placed it in my rucksack with an emergency teabag. If all got too much for me, if the doubt started to eat away at my insides, I would stop and make a brew (keep calm and put the kettle on!) and read through what people had written about me. Although I was thousands of miles away, at that precise moment those people would be with me, spurring me on, and to this day that small piece of paper is in my wallet ready to deploy should the depression hit hard.

Perhaps ultra running has given me the reason never to have to use it. By taking on a big challenge you will learn something about yourself. Ultra running has saved me from the pits of depression, and while I am still fighting it, I also know I have strength deep down inside me that got me through the MdS – and it is this that will help you get through some of the tougher parts of life as well.

Normal People Can Apply

'Sorry, you're really quite normal!'

With those words Dr Howard Hurst of the University of Central Lancashire sports science department finally crushed all the preconceptions I'd been building up for years about how finely tuned and extraordinary my running body really was. All those hours of training, the merciless interval sessions, the early mornings through the dark and wind and rain, the lung-bursting hills, the 'death or glory' killer workouts: and for what? Ordinary. Average. Normal.

It's January 2012 and I'm at the University Central Lancashire in north-west England for some physiological testing and playing ultra runner guinea pig. Specifically this involves sitting in a sealed space capsule being hydro-statically measured (body composition, weight via air displacement), having blood drawn (is it really good stuff in there?) and gurning and grunting on a treadmill (run at a set speed, the incline increasing incrementally as oxygen intake and use is measured – then we keep going beyond our max point just to see how big our *cojones* are).

After the disease-ridden December we had in our household I finally caved in as January approached, which has meant gentle activity at most for the last few weeks. It shows, and I'm appalled to find I can't exceed a predicted maximum heart rate on the test as I have done previously, and flounder pathetically off the whirring belt knowing it hasn't been a 100 per cent effort. Quite small ones, today then …

Ah well, at least we have an accurate starting point.

The good doctor is, however, somewhat intrigued …

'For someone who is clearly very fit and performing at the top of their game, your values – and I don't want to upset you – are very good, but not as high as we would have expected. Which means that there's something else in your make-up that makes the difference to your performance … could be related to economy in some way, could be lactate clearing, but I'll have to have a think …'

Well, my mum would say I'm just a stubborn so-and-so, but that's another story. Or is it? Because what we have here is science saying that there's a gap between what I should be doing, and what I actually *am* doing between the start and the finish line. And what I *am* doing is in excess of what science predicts.

This, then, is good news for all us ordinary mortals, in that having the physical capacity is important – but it doesn't have to be off the scale, and it's not the be all and end all: it means that other (non running?) factors are also at work. It's what we do with what we've got which is the key, and on this evidence, you can do a lot with what most people have – as long as you have the wit and motivation to do so.

What This Book Is – and Isn't

I've been endurance racing since I was a teenager, ultra running since 2003, and coaching professionally since 2000. I'm no scientist, so if you've picked this book up looking for facts, figures and controlled research – then I'm sorry, but it's not that kind of book. Neither is it a balanced and comprehensive work: it's my take on the subject, and that means there will probably be stuff that has you nodding, stuff that you raise your eyebrows at, and stuff that's not included that you think should be. Ultimately, you could say it's biased.

It is, however, an evidence-based piece. It's just that the evidence is from my own experimentation, from training and coaching others – and from forty-seven years as a fully paid up and curious member of the human race. There are some references and credits in here, but otherwise the stance I have taken on the subjects in this topic have been arrived at via my own curiosity, experience, influences, preferences and deductive reasoning.

Part of the reason for that is that it appears the science is just starting to get to grips with the exploding world of ultra running – I can find relatively few meaningful and conclusive studies (*see* the following section 'A Word About the Science') – and if science is playing 'catch-up', then why not turn the attention on to our own experience and those of the top boys and girls currently almost continuously poking holes in accepted beliefs and redefining the limits of the sport? We are, after all, all experts on ourselves – if we have the wit to ask the right questions.

Furthermore it really does appear to me that as the race distance increases, the less of a runner you need to be, and the less the normal rules of training and racing apply. Now if that's not a licence for experimentation and individual calibration, then I don't know what is.

There are no training plans in here, either. That's because I've no idea what a great training plan for you looks like. The only person that truly does is you – you're the expert, remember? Oh, there are some principles, assertions and beliefs in these pages that I'll argue hold true, and some examples of practical applications that drive the point home – but the only real way to figure out whether they are of any value for *you* is to have the courage to experiment and pay close attention to the results you get.

I've pulled my own conclusions, and while you may not agree with all of what you read here, if it at least prompts you to think differently about your own stuff, then I figure this book will have served a purpose.

A Word About the Science

The thing about research and hypotheses is that you can generally find what you're looking for – eventually. Now there's a whole host of reasons as to why this might be so, but to go there we'd be flirting with neurology, psychology and even the wonderful world of quantum physics – and we're not even past the first chapter of this book yet. Just know that we *generally get what we focus on* – more of this later – and that there's data out there that can be found to support almost any position. (As someone once said to me: 'Statistics are like a woman in a bikini – the interesting parts are always hidden.')

You also need to consider the origin and funding of the research, any vested interest the author may have in the outcome, and whether the terms of study are really relevant. (I've come across studies where a two-hour run was used to study 'endurance': fair enough, but that's a world of difference away from 'ultra', wouldn't you say?)

Many steps have been taken on the journey to writing this book. Some have been an uphill slog; and others ...

These are some of the reasons I've *not* sought to scientifically support every assertion I make here. Another is that quite frankly I got frustrated trying to find what I considered to be robust, objective, conclusive ultra running-specific stuff. It does exist, and I reference some works here. By contrast, my own field research has taken place over some three decades, and while my structured curiosity only really became habitual since 2000, that's still a considerably longer period of time than any other experiment I can find. And *that* I am prepared to defend, even if I also recognize that it's still a 'work in progress'.

Can We Build Ultra-running Perfection?

- What are the distiguishing features of an ultra runner?
- What are the key qualities and skills required?
- What am I striving for in my training?

In coaching it's good professional practice to start at the end – to examine the demands of the challenge ahead, and to come up with a shopping list of requirements to meet that challenge. This technical template then becomes the script for coach and athlete to design a training programme that bridges the gap from where the athlete is now, to where they need to be to meet that challenge. (That's right, you heard me – coach *and* athlete: in my world it's a collaborative thing because that promotes ownership, and ownership mean stickability, and stickability translates into consistency – and that, dear reader, is part of the platform for improvement.)

So I figured it made sense to start with the end in mind and to present you at the outset with my version of a technical template for ultra running. You won't even need to read the rest of this book – just grab a brew and play compare/contrast with your own strengths and weaknesses against those qualities required for ultra-running success listed below. Then go out and train to bridge the gap: simple! Mind you, that would be a shame because you'd miss all the rest of the great stuff I worked so hard to put together for you in this book … Still, it is 2014, and Attention Deficit Disorder is apparently on the rise, so if you really do want to cut to the chase then here it is …

Mental

Tactically astute – strategically aware – learning mentality

You have to be able to juggle lots of stuff in ultras: lots of stuff that happens lots of times because you're out there for longer than most people would consider normal. You have to balance a 'big picture' perspective (get to the finish line) with short-term or immediate choices (do I stop and put another layer on now, or …). There are so many variables to manage that frustration and disappointment are a normal part of the learning curve – how many of us can keep every plate spinning all of the time? – and every race really *is* unique, and that makes meaningful comparisons tough. Adopting a mindset in which the lessons from every experience are at least as important as the outcome will allow you to enjoy the process more and figure out your own success formula over time. Then you really are sorted.

Emotional

Self-awareness – perspective – emotional maturity

In order to be able to manage your mood for an extended period of time in challenging and variable circumstances you need to know your own triggers:

- What drives you?
- What flips you?
- What are the warning signs?

While you'll be on the start line with a bunch of other folks, it's also highly likely that for a good part of the race you'll be flying solo with no one to key off, distract you or dig you out of a hole. How resilient you are is key to coping with the challenges of the trail:

- How do you choose to respond to setbacks?
- How do you use the little victories?
- And how can you keep doing this time and time after time …?

It's also highly likely that few of your co-workers will understand what you do for kicks, and why you do it. This means that for you, the Monday morning 'So what did you do at the weekend?' conversation is probably going to be a very short one. Finding your own community is part of the journey, as is knowing what to get worked up about and what to let slide. This is a crucial filter to have mid-race, and also quite useful in life. Sure, this running ultras game is important to us who aspire do it – life-enhancing even – and it's also just running – isn't it?

Physical

Feet

Feet must be bombproof, elastic, and with toenails optional, while the owner – that's you – must have the skill and motivation to look after them day to day, and to conduct emergency repairs while out on the trail.

Legs

For legs, downhill-proof is arguably the biggest single requirement for the largest muscle group in the body. The quads take the biggest pounding, so learning how to descend smoothly and swiftly while preserving the integrity of the muscles is a skill to be acquired – as is a conditioning regime for your legs that a mountain goat would envy.

Torso

The ability to hold efficient posture over an extended period of time in a challenging and changing environment seems like a common sense requirement. Yet I continue to see far too many runners with truly awful posture, and not just in the final quarter of a race. No wonder it feels hard work if you're practically doubled up! This requirement becomes even more important with the trend to race packs and race vests – *you're operating under load, for crying out loud* – and especially so for runners taking part in multi-day ultras. The goal is to hold an upright torso – hips to shoulder – and that takes a little more than performing a floor plank exercise twice a week.

Movement Efficiency

Movement efficiency means maximum performance for the least amount of effort: the distinction between walking and running starts to blur as the race distances increase and the terrain gets rougher. Thinking about *covering the ground* as opposed to just *running* increases your locomotion choices by making any combination of walk-run you can think of an utterly legitimate option. Momentum is the aspirational state of being, and practically, this means that many runners can usefully spend time learning how to walk and power-hike

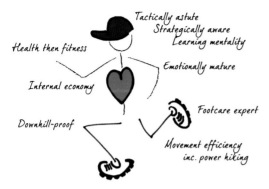

Ultra-running: a technical template.

effectively. If the difference between a fast hike and a slow run on rough terrain is 1 mile per hour but trying to run *feels* so much harder … it's a no-brainer, but only if you have trained to walk.

Heart and Lungs

Heart and lungs should be a model for economy so that you can do what you want to do without really being aware that you're doing it.

Health then Fitness

Building a healthy whole unit on which to add ultra-running fitness is a route to longevity in a sport that is essentially repetitive strain injury writ large. You will, I'm sure, know runners who are fit as a fiddle but fundamentally unhealthy – walking a tighrope from race to race prone to injury and illness. This model puts you on the start line healthy *first* and fit second so you have reserves to draw on during and after the event: race long and recover stronger – what is there not to like in this?

Six Things you should Know before you Start

1. It's Not About the Distance

In my experience most runners stepping up to ultra distance running think it's all about the distance. Don't get me wrong, the distance is what defines this sport – we are captivated by tales of people covering huge distances over big terrain at incredible speeds, and what they go through to get to the finish line – but for me, the distance on its own is not the issue.

Here's what I think: *I think that anyone can put this book down right now and head out and cover 100 miles – if you're motivated enough, that is.* Now there's also a lot of stuff around self-management, and you will need to be able to practise the skills of perseverance; but the good news is that these can be learned – and if you strip everything else away I think there's just one thing left: leverage.

If you did head out, here's what I think would happen:

• Some of you would take far longer than others
• Some of you would be in a box at the end
• And some of you would take an age to recover the desire to do any weight-bearing activity again

So I put it to you one more time: as long as you were motivated enough I think you'd all get there. Eventually.

So if it really isn't about the distance, why is it normal that so many people fail to finish an ultra? And that proportionally more men will fail to finish than women? Some of the bigger mountain races have a start-to-finish ratio of

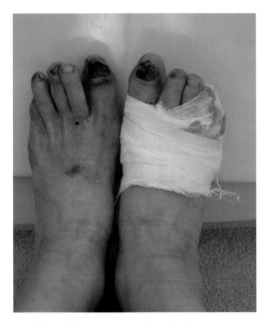

Feet – if they had workers' rights, we'd be in serious trouble!

We'll examine these in more detail later; for now it's enough to start from the position that the distance *per se* is not a limiting factor.

2. Normal Rules Don't Seem to Apply

You see, in ultra running it's my belief that many of the normal rules (of training and racing) don't apply. So if that's the case, the *only* way to figure out the rules that apply to you is to experiment – and *that* means being prepared to be knocked back in the short term. Look around any start line and you'll see people of all shapes, sizes and ages – yet shape, size and age doesn't seem to correlate with a DNF. At the top end of the sport it's the young guns who are setting the world alight – which is strange, because isn't this distance lark supposed to a game for the old 'uns? And then there's nutrition: I know people who compete on junk food and those who exist on gels – and both seem to get the results they want: so what's that about?!

There is indeed some specific research out there, but because this modern incarnation (see note* below) of ultra running is relatively recent, much of the research is inconclusive. What you have here are my conclusions based on patterns and trends I've observed in my own journey, and for the people I coach and meet through my speaking and training.

A bottom line is that while there is a stack of consensus and training manuals about how to prepare for, and race, marathon and triathlon, the same cannot be said of ultra running. As I write, the curious among us in the world of ultra running/research are still searching for consensus on the following topics:

around 2:1 – that's right, one out of two people will not reach the finish line.

If we take the assertion above, then there's clearly something about focus, desire and managing mood – but as you'll see later, there also comes a point in ultras where no amount of Jedi mind tricks will keep you moving. Right at the extreme end of prolonged exertion the brain – charged as it is with self-preservation and maintaining homeostasis – will simply press the reset button and shut the body down. So on that basis there clearly is something physiological as well.

And then there's the business end: your feet. There's no shortage of pictures in books, magazines and on line of mashed and trashed extremities – usually accompanied by screaming and crying on behalf of the owner, and often by a Did Not Finish (DNF). So there's clearly something about foot care and shoe choice as well.

- The long training run
- The best race food
- The role of speed training
- What an effective taper looks like
- What recent gear innovations really do make a difference

What research there is is patchy, and much of it concludes – at least in part – that more research is needed.

Personally, I find that incredibly liberating – but that's just me: I also know plenty of people who have come into the sport with a proscriptive approach to training and racing, and have got incredibly frustrated before they realize that that model has limited applicability at best. Yes, of course there are some black-and-white absolutes – for some of you extended time on your feet can make a real difference to the chances of success – and there are also many shades of grey. I will do my best to tread that line, and give you the material that I have found really makes a difference. To reiterate: this is not an 'a + b = c' book – though there are indeed scenarios where that does hold … See what I mean?!

* Mass participation trail ultra running is a new beast, but the Victorians were pounding the boards and roads long before 'the running shoe' appeared, and in the UK some of the records that were set in the 1950s and 1960s by the hard road men of that era bear comparison even today.

3. Compound and Cumulative

What big distance does is introduce the compound and cumulative effect. In other words, it's never just one thing happening at just one time: there's usually lots of things happening at the same time over and over again, and which will keep happening all the way till the finish. Stuff that can be ignored or cut short over the shorter distances can't be ignored over the longer distance – so that little hotspot on your foot could well develop into a raw, bleeding mess if you keep pounding, and will be a problem all race long unless you stop and deal with it in the early stages.

The little things are always easier to deal with than the big ones, and one way of keeping them little is to take action early. To do *that* means having your wits about you, paying attention, having good personal organization, and being 'on task' – which of course is significantly easier to do in the early stages of a race when the effort is easy and the happy tank is full. As the race goes on, more effort is required to keep putting one foot in front of the other, which means less energy is available for anything else. Throw in some bad weather, a night of missed sleep, and even vaguely competitive inclinations, and suddenly what was a simple action at mile ten becomes a problem of seemingly insurmountable proportions eight, ten or twenty hours later.

So the distance on its own is not the issue. What the distance does is extend the playing time – which means that little stuff will build to big stuff, and one thing will get added to by another, and another and another. Think spinning plates, of which there's only ever one outcome: eventually one of them will fall …

I Know This Because ...

My first 100-miler was the iconic Western States Endurance Run in the USA in 2005, and I went into it physically under-prepared. I knew that – and I figured I had what it took mentally and emotionally to finish. I was right, but the final third was one of the most painful, humbling and draining experiences I've ever had. One of my most vivid recollections came during the night heading towards mile ninety when I came to a juddering halt at the edge of a small stream. My legs were so shot I couldn't work out how to move them differently out of pathetic shuffle-stumble mode and into stream-crossing mode. It just didn't occur to me for ages that it was OK to get my feet wet. I remember being reduced to tears of frustration rooted to the spot as I simply could *not* work out how to get going again.

4. Performance is Emotional

Preparation and training are basically task oriented in that you just have to do the work – except that having a great work ethic is no guarantee that you'll reach the finish line. Performance, on the other hand – racing – is a very different animal, and the difference on any given day, all things being equal, will be *how you feel*. Or more specifically, how you *choose* to feel. Put any group of athletes together on a start line who have used the same training plan and have similar training histories and dietary patterns, and the winner will be the one who harnesses their emotions and manages their mood to greatest effect.

So the only question that's worth asking is this: *how can you plan how you need to feel in order to have the race you want?*

We've already seen the impact of *compound and cumulative* over ultra distance: there's no faking, no bluffing – you can't just gut it out. Mood swings, doubt, elation, distraction are all normal, and because of the huge distance involved the chances are that you'll be dealing with them time and time again. You'll see later on that as the race distance increases so does the requirement and skill to manage your emotions. Your defence is not simply the number of miles you've covered in training – it's something else entirely:

- What you say to yourself
- What you picture in your mind
- What you choose to focus on
- How ready you are to accept 'failure' as a learning step
- How much leverage you have, and how much it matters to finish

This is the stuff the training plans don't tell you – because it's training, not racing – and racing is emotional. And don't sit there and tell me that because you're not at the sharp end this doesn't apply to you: just because someone takes double the amount of time to cover a course as the winner doesn't make them any less of a competitor. As someone else once said: '*The hardest competitor you will ever race against is yourself.*'

Everything is relative, and in the final analysis it all comes down to this: if the hardest competitor any of us will ever face is really ourselves, it makes sense to have something to compete with, don't you think?

5. Confidence is the Currency

The right training plan for you is one that builds confidence. This means that whatever you need to do to feed that feeling is the right thing for you. To be sure, a smart training plan is one that starts with the target race in mind, and marries your relative strengths and weaknesses with the demands of the event. It can be a work of technical genius at the cutting edge of the latest ultra research – but if it doesn't spark you up and build a 'can do – am doing – will do' attitude, you're only getting half the deal.

You need to be on that start line with a high degree of self-belief, and carry a mindset that makes it easy for you to choose to pay attention during the event to those indicators that feed your feeling of progress and reassure you that you are at least equal to the task ahead. That means taking note of stuff like this:

- How far you've come
- How good you're feeling
- How you're enjoying your surroundings

REVELATIONS FROM REAL RUNNERS

Confidence is the Currency

Sharon McDonald

What have I learnt? If the weather is extreme, then it's extreme for everyone! All ultra racers go through a stage of feeling very sick and physically drained, not just me. The biggest thing is how *you* learn what works for you to get through and to keep going when the going gets tough. I think of what I've already done, then compare it, and whether it's up there with the gnarly ones or not, the thinking is the same: *Hey! Get on with it!* You've done it before, and if it's the hardest thing yet, then tell yourself it's time for that new benchmark to be set because you want to progress – well, it's worked for me so far. Nothing lasts for ever, and if there is an easy option then I do the opposite because I'm very, very stubborn (just ask my other half).

Now like any addict, I have to have more adventures and goals, I know I can do more, so what next? The Lakeland 100, the Bob Graham Round, UTMB … the journey just keeps getting better and longer.

6. A Change is as Good as a Rest

Think of ultramarathon running as repetitive strain injury writ large – which means if you've only got one way of doing it – *you just run* – you're going to break down pretty quickly unless you are very special ultra-running animal. These do exist, but they are quite rare – even the top boys and girls rarely run the whole way on a long mountain race.

The key is to have lots of slightly different ways to make relentless forward motion. This gives you choices and options – *this is powerfulness* – and this means you can change/rest as you go along without completely exhausting one method of travel. I remember leading one coaching camp out in the French Alps where we came up with seven different ways of getting up a hill:

- Running
- Running with very small steps
- Walking
- Walking with trekking poles
- Walking with long strides and exaggerated arm swings
- Walking pushing the hands down on top of the thighs with every step
- Taking a zig-zag route

You get the idea. What this means is that you can change your mode of travel to match the terrain, how you feel, and tactically what you want to happen. Every time you change something you are resting something else:

- Switch to walking? Your running muscles take a break
- Use your poles? You take some of the weight off your feet
- Reduce your stride length? You feel more relaxed, which allows you to back off

This also applies literally. A change of clothes from a dropbag or support crew mid-race can be incredibly revitalizing. My own favourite if the weather is hot is to go full emersion in a stream for a few seconds – the equivalent of pressing a reset button. Small personal rituals can also have the same effect: brushing your teeth after ten to twenty hours scoffing all sorts of stuff can border on orgasmic release – apparently.

The point is to be constantly fine-tuning, changing something – even if that's just the tension on a rucksack or bumbag strap – in the same way a yacht skipper would be continually trimming the boat to get consistent performance even in settled conditions. Resting in ultras is fine, but the clock is ticking and sometimes a change will do the job just as well.

In Summary

- The race distance on its own is not a limiting factor
- The greater the race distance, the greater the compound and cumulative effect
- Performance is about how you feel: it's *not* about how good your training has been
- Motivation will only get you part way
- The normal rules of training don't seem to apply
- Expect to experiment
- Pay attention: the secrets of your success and failures will be in your diary
- Keep a diary – about your life
- As the race distance increases, the more you need skills to manage how you feel
- Training is all about building confidence
- Competing is about managing confidence
- Focus on you and your stuff
- Choose *powerfulness*: have more than one way of competing
- Ultrarunning is RSI
- Change and variety will keep you moving and keep repetitive strain injury at bay

Ultra Running Made Ultra Simple

The following section investigates what it takes to reach the finish line.

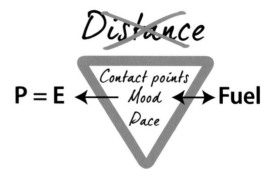

What does it take to reach the finish line? Copy this out and stick it to your fridge door.

It's Not About the Distance

- If you're motivated enough you can go the distance
- The distance gives you *compound* and *cumulative* to deal with
- The greater the distance, the less of a pure runner you need to be

What It Is About

Keeping your Contact Points Intact
- Ultra running is a contact sport and repetitive strain writ large
- Blisters, rubbing and chafing can seriously ruin your day
- Pro- and re-activity for footcare and wear, pack and bag carrying points

If you're motivated enough, you can go the distance.

Controlling your Pace and Minimizing Impact:

- Most men go too fast, too early
- Even pace makes a (happy) finish more likely, and women do even pace better
- More pace needs more energy, and mismanaging your energy levels affects *everything*

Managing your Mood:

- You need to be the expert on *you*
- Performance is emotional (P=E)
- Confidence is the currency

Is it Really that Simple?

I've already stated that this book is based on my experience and therefore it represents a particular perspective. I've also stated that I think science is really only just getting started on this subject. Of the science that there is, the most comprehensive studies on ultramarathon running I can find started years ago around the Western States Endurance Run – the premier 100-mile trail ultra race in the USA. The WS Research Group are still using the race participants as guinea pigs today. Here in the UK, Dr Sam Robson piloted some research based on the 2012 South Downs Way 100 miler to look at the factors affecting performance and finish rates.

For the record, I've had my *Ultra Running Made Ultra Simple* template since 2010, and the first time that I compared it to any meaningful science was in preparation for this book. I've pulled what I can from both the sources mentioned above so you can see what some of the science says about what ultra running is and isn't.

Common Characteristics of Ultra Runners on the Finish Line

- Motivated by challenge
- Don't run 'excessively' long in training*
- Use even-pace strategy (as close as possible), which makes for a slightly faster overall time
- Even pace (as close as …) makes for a happier racing experience
- They are older
- There are proportionally more women. They are thoroughly prepared (i.e. in personal organization, training time, the way they manage expectations)

* Runners who covered an average of fifty miles in one outing for a 100-mile race were more likely not to finish.

On this basis it would appear that if you are older, female, up for a challenge, have come into the race healthy, without running mega miles, have thought about it and are prepared, and have just run even pace ... we are more likely to see you at the finish of a 100-mile trail ultra.

Next we will look at the flip side and those who – according to these studies – start and are less likely to finish.

Common Characteristics of Ultra Runners by the Wayside

- Carry an old injury
- Run 'excessively' long distances in training
- Start the race fast
- Are young
- Are male
- Suffer significant muscle pain mid-race
- Try running fast in hot conditions

The flip side of the flip side is that over the last few years there are also more young people ripping up the sport. Some of these will indeed start fast, run mega miles in training, be hardly affected by heat, and are highly motivated to suffer. But these, I suggest, are the exceptions, and there will always be some for the rest of us to marvel at: what we are talking about here are us mere mortals, likelihoods and *probabilities* ...

In Summary

- It's not about the distance
- The distance just means you have more stuff to deal with more often, and for longer
- As the distance increases the less of a runner you need to be
- All you need to start is to be up for a challenge
- Keep your points of contact intact
- Control your pace
- Minimize your impact
- Energy depletion has physical, mental and emotional consequences
- Manage your mood
- Performance is emotional
- Confidence is the currency
- Even-pace running is a route to happiness
- Women do even-pace running better
- Don't leave your racing in your training miles
- Be on the start line healthy
- Think about it all – thoroughly

Knowing When You're Ready

Many runners ask how they will know when they're ready for their first ultra. My reply is: *'If you're motivated enough to fill out an entry form, you're ready: everything else is just detail.'*

'What sort of race should I start with?' asked one of my audience members a few years ago.

I replied, 'Start with something that inspires you.'

Now that's quite a wide remit, and some way different from a typical progression of, say, marathon–50km–40 miles–50 miles. Think about it this way: you'll be out there for a very long time. If you're in a new place that you're curious about with cool scenery – in other words, plenty of reasons to be distracted – then the odds are that it'll make the miles pass more easily. And if the miles seem to pass more easily then you are starting to load the dice in favour of a finish.

The great thing about getting into the sport now is that there are more and more races happening in more and more places, and many of them take you into locations that will make you smile on the inside and out. You just need to have the wit to take note.

So enter something that grabs you. If you have that, then you'll also be motivated to train. All that remains is to prepare with the goal in mind, and to make that preparation an experience that adds to the quality of your life – as opposed to becoming another source of stress. Or if you want to simplify it even more, do stuff that you *enjoy*, and stuff that builds *confidence* (Matt Fitzgerald, 2007). Anything else is just fluffy packing.

... you're ready for this.

If this moves you ...

REVELATIONS FROM REAL RUNNERS

Making It Matter

Sarah Sheridan

If I tell someone I'm going to do something, I usually do it. Not to do it is to fail, in my book. Not always a healthy approach, but a successful one for me when it comes to training and racing.

When I decided to do my first ultra I had a higher objective in mind, one which I only shared with my significant other who calmly tolerates my madness and is himself an endurance athlete of the cycling kind. This higher objective remains undisclosed to most of my friends and family as I am not yet convinced I can achieve it. Running ultras is the means I am using to determine whether this objective is achievable!

I tell my friends and family about the ultras I am going to do, so am in training for, and in racing ultras I have an unhealthy compulsion (to do what I say I am going to do) and a probably unrealistic goal that keeps me going. When I am in late from work and have a ten-mile training run to do in the dark, it's snowing, I'm tired and all the other things that aren't getting done are gnawing away at me, I remind myself of my higher goal, the expectation of my friends and family, and most of all the feeling of elation when my fitness allows me to run for hours through breathtaking mountain landscapes in all weathers with my dog for company. And afterwards, to be back home with my husband when we can chat about our experiences over a bowl of pasta and burning legs.

Geoff Cox

Every time I think about the sheer improbability of running 100 miles I think of the gravel voice of Ken Chlouber, the energy behind the Leadville 100: 'The biggest distance to conquer in this race is five inches, the five inches between your ears; if you can't control that ... you're dead meat.'

Everybody tells you about the mental strength it takes to be an ultra runner, and I'd always believed they meant the grit to take another step, the drive to start running again after you've been forced to walk, the ability to bury the pain down deep so that it doesn't equate to a DNF.

Now I realize that the strength needed is a whole lot bigger than that: it's the strength to make running vitally important in your life, so important that you're not going to compromise it for pretty much anything, and this is a condition that needs to permeate every atom of your body and soul for years and years.

So, how important is it to me? What am I prepared to give up to achieve my potential as a runner, and what am I *not* prepared to give up? I'm fifty-eight, successful at my job, I've surrounded myself with the benefits of that success... yet I can't make the commitment to be good at what I love?... Really?

If I don't do it now I'll be too old to make a go of it, I'm going to die wondering 'What if?'. This cycle of failure and disappointment is going to happen over and over again, every year until I hang up my shoes, I'll go straight from 'wannabe' to 'never was' without ever having experienced 'that year it all came together'.

So how much do you want it, Geoff? How much are you prepared to put on the line?

So we sat down one evening, my wife and I and a sheet of paper that slowly filled up with figures. I squirmed under questioning – I didn't have the answers, but I had something else: a deep, fundamental, visceral need to be all that I could be as a runner, and slowly that became more important than the numbers. I wrote the resignation mail and pressed 'Send'.

Then came the waves of emotion... exposure, vulnerability, pure fear... and all wrapped in a knowledge that this was one of the happiest days of my life.

Now I'm starting to understand what they mean by mental strength: it starts with the belief that you *can* run an ultra marathon, but the true test is having the courage to become an ultra runner.

CHAPTER 2

Making the Transition

Marathon to Ultra Marathon

You can't bluff in an ultra – ignore your basics and the warning signs at your peril. The things you can get away with over 26.2 miles can seriously compromise your performance, and even cause you to DNF over forty, fifty and a hundred miles. That hotspot on the ball of your foot? Stop and sort it out before it develops into a bad blister that has you crying a few miles later when you still have thirty miles to go. That flapping, noisy, ill-fitting kit? It will drive you to distraction, and that means a waste of valuable mental energy. That sense of humour failure? Probably means you need to eat and drink. Over 100 miles, 'mind over matter' is a myth. Neglect your fuelling and your body will ultimately shut down and you will *stop*.

Know Your Place

You need to be able to navigate in an ultra, and whole/part route recces in advance of race day are invaluable. If you are confident in where you are /where you are going, then you have more mental and emotional energy to give to the task of relentless forward motion – which is, after all, the basis of ultra-marathon running success.

This does not mean being a whiz with a compass: there are things you can do before you even get outside just by turning the route info provided by race organizers into a format that works for you. Prefer lists rather than maps? Translate the map info into a route card of your preferred size and detail, and bigger than normal font size. Then stick it in a plastic sleeve and seal the sleeve. Run holding the card with your thumb always on your present/next route feature.

Night Time is the Right Time

You will need to be comfortable running at night in an ultra. It's a different skill set for a different sensory experience. Many of your usual indicators of progress will be missing – the view ahead, for example. Learning to relax and enjoy the beauty and challenges of running at night can transform your ultra running. A way to start is to go out on familiar trails with a good light – minimalist lights are all well and good, but first and foremost you want to see where you are going, right? – and with friends. This will give you other people to key off and focus on, apart from '*Oh, look how dark and spooky it is, and I can't seem to see where my feet are going*'.

Know Thyself

An ultra requires greater levels of self-awareness and greater skills in self-management. Why? Because success will ultimately depend on managing how you feel, over an extended period of time when you are being constantly challenged in a constantly changing environment to make good on a big commitment.

There's nothing like your own company for twelve to twenty-four hours as a way of getting up close and personal with the real you. Though self-knowledge is, of course, only half the story – you then need to have the motivation and skill to act on that knowledge when the situation demands it, *and* do so in a way that is helpful.

Which means making a decision. That's right, your decision-making skills also get a workout. Of course, decisions only have meaning in the context of a clear and compelling goal – which means dusting off your goal-setting skills as well. Sorry.

It's OK to Walk

You will need to train to walk for an ultra. Even the top boys and girls walk at some point in the long races – though you wouldn't think so from their incredible times! For us mere mortals this falls into two categories: flats and climbs.

Walking efficiently in a race is a world away from your usual amble to the shops, and is therefore a skill to be practised. Walking gives you a physical and mental moving break, and in ultras a break really *can* be as good as a rest.

It Isn't Over if You Blow

You can blow up and recover fully in an ultra – really … Even if you lie down and have a little sleep because it's all getting a bit too much.

What's thirty minutes over twelve or twenty-four hours? Go back to 'Know Thyself', and know what to do when this happens. Here's a brief checklist:

• Know the signs
• Heed the signs
• Slow down, walk, eat and drink – let everyone else go – you'll see them later
• Reduce the size of the chunk of the race you are focused on
• Talk good stuff to yourself
• Be patient as the fuel goes to work
• Change something else if you need to be really sure
• Keep talking – have faith
• Re-start slowly, telling yourself how clever you are!
• It's OK to sleep on the job

It is usually preferable to sleep under supervision at an aid station – though I do know people who just couldn't wait and crashed out in the undergrowth. But this is risky and it scares the tourists. Set an alarm on your watch, or tell a member of the aid-station crew what you are doing – there are few things more alarming to a volunteer than to discover a body at their checkpoint – and ask them to wake you at a time of your choice.

Be in the Present

It can be more helpful to focus on the journey rather than a destination in an ultra, not least because the final destination tends to be a very long way ahead – so far ahead sometimes, that we can barely get our head around it. So focus on the things you can control, get your head up and enjoy the moment – which is, after all, unique. Helpfully, most ultras take you through beautiful landscapes, which means there's much to enjoy and take in if you have the wit to do so.

If The End is a very, *very* long way away, then it can be spectacularly unhelpful to focus on how far away it is and how long you need to travel to get there. That's the deal you signed up to when you paid the entry, and it isn't going to change.

Black and White versus Shades of Grey

It can be more helpful to focus on subjective rather than objective measures. This can be quite a challenge, because much of marathon preparation and racing is around splits and heart rate and mile markers and training zones and minute-per-mile pace, and 'the wall' at twenty miles. Absolutes where it either 'is', or 'is not'.

In ultras there are so many factors to juggle with over such a long time that giving yourself a mental break and room to *manoeuvre* just becomes good sense, as well as helping you enjoy the journey. Hitting absolute indicators time and time again can become a very stress-ful way to operate, whereas managing how you feel suddenly opens up a whole new world – because we do this for free, right?

Decisions, Decisions

An ultra requires that you really are a good/decisive decision-maker. Know thyself.

Wish You Were Here

You get more/more of inspiring landscapes in an ultra. Unless your thing is going to be those twenty-four-hour track races, of course.

I know of few things more effective at taking your mind away from the miles than the majesty of Mother Nature. And before you think I'm going to turn tree-hugger on you, think on this: I'm not talking about rubber-necking through a car window. You will be part of those landscapes with all the sensory experience to go with it. Areas that you think you know will take on many more shades of meaning once you have your own journey to thread through them.

I Want to be Alone

You have a greater chance of running alone during part of an ultra. Yes, the field size is growing as more and more people go longer and go off road, but the probability remains: you will need to be cool with your own com-pany and confident in your ability to motivate and look after yourself. Unless you are racing in the States or Europe you are unlikely to be regaled at regular intervals by cheering crowds and a manic MC. We are, after all, the repressed English. Practise the art of self-reliance, dear reader.

Get Sorted

Personal organization is vital: you need to get the 'faff factor' to a minimum, because if it's a faff, forty miles into a fifty-mile race when you're not thinking straight, you'll not do something – and that could be end of race for you.

A reason many people don't/can't navigate? It's a faff doing all that stuff with a map. A reason many people have problems with blisters and chafing? It's a faff stopping, getting the kit out and doing the repairs on crappy feet. The reason a good friend of mine had dehydration problems on nearly every race was because it was a faff to reach his drink bottles stashed on his rucksack.

In ultras, personal organization is (nearly) everything. Test, refine, and test your kit choices and equipment stash locations till you can reach/do nearly everything while on the move. If it's simple and easy you'll do/use it – if it isn't, you won't.

When You Gotta Go ...

You need to be comfortable with a wide range of toilet skills and locations. One of my most vivid recollections from my early ultra days was racing in the US and seeing a lady runner peeing successfully from a standing position just a few yards off the path. She just hoiked her shorts to one side and ... you have a picture, I'm sure.

You should expect to have to go. Physical effort plus mental stress, plus often strange foods, plus miles and miles can play havoc with your insides. The only way to find out which foods agree with you – and this could differ according to effort level and how hot it is – is

to experiment. You might have to go through some unexpected and messy results before figuring this out. So carry your toilet paper in a little plastic bag (*see* faff factor above): please.

The general etiquette is to go away from the path and bury it, or bag it and take it with you. Some races are specific: at UTMB in France all runners are given a mesh bag which can be threaded to a waistbelt for litter and toilet paper to be disposed of at checkpoints. As environmental awareness becomes more mainstream, our racing footprints will be required to be ever lighter.

Compounded and Complicated

There are more and different factors to plan for/deal with in an ultra. Some of the differences I'm covering here. Then we also have the compounding effect, and that is simply a function of the greater distance. Thus there are more aid stations. More kit to carry, as you're out for more time. More choices to make. More food to eat. More drink to drink. More weather to deal with. More time to think. More stuff to forget. More opportunities to give up. All this just because there are many, many more miles to go.

Train to Get Down

You really need to train for the descents. It's the downhills that are the quad killer, and if your upper legs are exhausted then it's pretty much hobble time from there on in. Remember the compound effect? This is where you pay with interest.

Descending effectively and efficiently is a different skill set from, say, the full-on styles seen in shorter fell races in the north of England. In ultras the emphasis is on conservation and preservation of the muscles and the energy systems. This means the technique is different.

And if you don't have hills to train on? Move house. If you can't move house, then help is at hand because there is plenty of stuff you can do in a gym and outside to condition those quads.

The Normal Rules do not Apply

Be prepared to experiment – the normal rules do not seem to apply over the big distances. Ever wonder why there is a stack of 'How to train for the marathon' books, and relatively little choice for ultras? Because the curious among us are still figuring it out, and much of the research is still fairly inconclusive. Sure, there is some consensus, and that is to *run*. 'Run as often as you can – and run' is the standout one for me in Tim Noakes' *Lore Of Running.*

But after that? Heck, I know people who race off junk foods and others who have nothing but gels. I know people whose long run is all day, and others who achieve on two hours. Listen, if it gets you the results you want in the way you want them and you can make those results stick over time – then whatever you're doing is a legitimate strategy for you. Even if it's totally different from the next guy and you can't find any mention of it in the manuals.

More Ultra Observations

Be Special
The field size is smaller for an ultra race. So that start line you're on and those people you're with? It's a pretty unique place and a special bunch of people.

Even one of the biggest ultras in the world, UTMB in France, has only 2,500 starters – which pales into insignificance alongside your average big city marathon.

Ultra-running is growing – but we've some way to go before we reach this scale!

Ladies: this Sport is for You!
Women get more cheers because there are fewer of them in the races, and those that are present perform relatively better over ultra-marathon distances. A higher proportion of women will finish than men, and the gaps between the top men and top women in the sport are very small and getting smaller. Women are winning ultras outright.

Finish First

The finish proportion of the field is smaller for an ultra race – much smaller. It's normal for one out of two people to DNF at the longer mountain races. Whatever your aspirations and level, remember this: you need to earn the right to finish first. Anything else is a bonus.

In Summary

- Preventative action is required: pay attention to, and act on, the warning signs
- You are your own navigator
- Embrace the night
- You really need to get to know *you*
- Walking is allowed
- Blowing up mid-race need not be terminal
- Sleeping is allowed
- Enjoy the journey because the destination is a long way away
- Dust off your decision-making skills
- Choose inspiring locations
- Be comfortable in your own company
- Get sorted
- More distance means more things to deal with more often
- Become downhill proof
- Be prepared to experiment – and be periodically frustrated
- Enjoy the learning
- Your success formula is your success formula, whatever anyone else says
- Women do it better
- First you have to finish – and a finish is special

Triathlon to Ultra Marathon

Embrace Simplicity

'It's just running, right?' This was an initial tongue-in-cheek response from a client of mine contemplating a change from the world of multi-sport. He was right – and despite the growing attempts of an increasing number of equipment manufacturers to make it more complicated, ultra running is a very simple sport:

> Put one foot in front of the other and keep doing that till you reach the finish line.

Now that's quite a change from three sports – two of which require high levels of technical skill to execute them well – two transitions, and a significantly fatter rule book. Think 'low tech' – you can even think 'no tech'. You will be entering a much simpler world – and you can be relieved, excited or intimidated by that.

More Head Space

Simpler, less to think about, so there is more room for the demons to come … How you fill your head is arguably even more of a challenge. You can't think about stroke counts or waves or drafting or transition sequence or gear ratios or pedal action because they're not there. It's just you, your feet and the course. I think there is an even greater requirement to be able to associate (think about the inside and the now) and disassociate (be away with the fairies), and to switch between the two.

You've got plenty of time to yourself during an ultra.

Boys and Toys

I say 'boys' because in my experience it is usually the lads who are drawn to the flashy, shiny gear – though I'm sure the fairer sex does have its examples … Anyhow, if you are into sport for its gadgets and gear, this is not the one for you. Sorry – though it is changing …

You Are Your Pillar of Support

You carry everything you need. There is no water to provide buoyancy or a very nice bicycle to drape your limbs around. So that beautifully sculpted upper body? Sorry, no real need.

Those ripped and bulging quads? Great for the hills and mountains, but over the flatter stuff? A bit excess to requirements. The bike-mounted bottles and food bags? Well, that lot will have to go round your waist or over your shoulders – because there's also probably fewer aid stations than you'll be used to. One of the simplest ways to go faster in this game is to get less and get lighter – that's you and your kit. Anything else is just excess baggage.

Buffed and Ripped

Buffed and ripped means that unless you are Dean Kanarzes – US ultra runner of note who is an inspiration to many – you are unlikely to be looking as much of a sex god as you did in your triathlon days. Your upper body will have withered, your quads will have deflated somewhat, your legs sprouted hairs, and your tan lines will be in different places. And your feet? Sorry, but they'll be trashed, and you'll view lost toenails as good news just because it's less weight to carry around.

RSI

You can think of ultra running as a recipe for repetitive strain injury writ large, which means that if you've only got one way of training – 'I'm just gonna run, dude' – the odds are that you're going to break something. Especially if you've come from a multi-sport background where it's easier to balance the strains of training.

You can find plenty of evidence – anecdotal and researched – about the running benefits accrued from cycling, for example. And the fact remains: fitness is specific, and if you want to get good at ultra running then you will need to run.

So if you ever figure out how to get the balance right, please let me know – because I'm still working on that one.

More Ultra Skills and Observations

Know your Place
You need to be able to navigate.

Night Time is the Right Time
You will need to be comfortable running at night.

Enjoy the Quiet
In ultra running there are fewer athletes per race, fewer spectators, no splashing of water, whirring of wheels or slap of feet on tarmac. The odds are that on quite a few occasions it will be just you, your surroundings, and whatever noise you bring along with you. And you can choose to see that either as a release and an opportunity, or as something else entirely.

Going Off Road

Unless you're planning to stay on the track or the tarmac, your feet are set for a very different running experience. Gone will be the lovely smooth roads and predominantly flat courses and straight line requirement. Say hello to mud, dust, rocks, moorland, pasture and race routes which twist and turn and take you high and low in equal measure.

If you are planning to go ultra and off-road your feet and ankles will need some help and some time to make a successful transition.

Your sense of anticipation, balance and coordination skills will also need sharpening up if you are to run easily and smoothly over rugged terrain that is constantly changing. It's a world away from the heavy-legged first few miles (or more) after 112 cycling miles where you're just crashing your feet down on to the pavement.

Know Thyself

An ultra requires greater levels of self-aware-ness and greater skills in self-management.

It's OK to Sleep on the Job

Even if you lie down and have a little sleep.

Black and White Versus Shades of Grey

It can be more helpful to focus on subjective rather than objective measures.

I Want to be Alone

You have a greater chance of running alone during part of an ultra.

When you Gotta Go …

You need to be OK with a wide range of toilet skills and locations. As a triathlete you should already have mastered the skill of peeing from a moving bike while maintaining good relations with your close (and draught-legal) competitors. So think of this as just widening your skill set.

The Normal Rules do not Apply

Be prepared to experiment because we're still writing the definitive training manual.

Be Special

This one's worth reiterating: the field size is smaller for an ultra race. So that start line you're on and those people you're with? It's quite a rare place, and quite a special bunch of people.

Women

This sport is for you.

You End up with More Money

No, really! The races cost less to enter, you have only one sport to kit out for, and you'll never pay excess baggage for your bike at an airport ever again. How cool is that?!

Finish First

The finishing proportion is small for an ultra race. Much smaller than Ironman. It's normal for one out of two people to DNF at the longer mountain races. Whatever your aspirations and level, remember this: you need to earn the right to finish first. Anything else is a bonus.

In Summary

- It's a simpler world with lower tech and far fewer toys
- There's less to think about and more time to think
- Get used to weight-bearing
- Farewell sex god
- Multi-sport to single sport: less margin for error
- Embrace the silence
- Going off road: it's back to school for feet and ankles
- Congratulations! You have reduced your costs

Jumping Right In

I know people with very little running history who have certainly not come through the 10km–half marathon–marathon progression, and who have jumped right into the trail ultrarunning scene. Yes, really.

Once again findings from the Western States Research Group back this up. 25 per cent of a study group (Hoffman MD, Krishnan E, 2013) had run an ultra within three years of starting regular running – and even more significant for race organizers in particular, this three-year window was reducing. In other words, a significant proportion of 'newbies' were jumping into ultras earlier and earlier, and part of the reason was that they started regular running at the median age of twenty-six.

'Newbies' start later – are highly motivated – and want to get on with it.

On the face of it that sounds like a route to disaster, and there is of course a flip side: these people will have less ultra-running experience to draw on in a sport where almost all the learning is by doing it. However, they are still alive and functioning, so clearly there's something else at work. Here's what I think that something is:

- It's not about the distance
- It might be something *big* that inspires you to start (*see* above)
- It's not really about the running

Let's take that last one. Unless you're at the top end of the field you won't be ultra-marathon *running* – you'll be ultra marathon *covering the*

ground as best you can. In other words there will be some walking with a bit of running thrown in. This is where many runners (usually blokes) come unstuck – they think it is about running so they commit two mistakes: they run as far as they can until they are reduced to a shuffle, and they neglect to practise walking efficently in their training.

As the race distance increases, the less of a runner you need to be.

Over the shorter distances (say, up to marathon distance) it's nearly all about the ability to run. You will need to be mentally alert – control your pace, remember to eat and drink – and there will be some *mood management* required, but by and large you can grit your teeth and get there if you want to. So most of the training is *running* and can be considered in the following order of importance:

1 Physical
2 Mental
3 Emotional

The Distance Makes the Difference

The picture changes for ultras, especially the big ones, when it's much more about tactics, strategy, being on task, managing mood, and *covering the ground* using a combination of walking and running and a combination of styles within those modes. In other words, you've got to think about it more. Yes, your working ends need to be physically robust, but that's a very different requirement to a pure running/racing snake, and might be considered as:

1   Mental
2   Emotional
3   Physical

What this means is that if you can walk efficiently for long distances at around 3–4mph on the flatter gradients, you've a perfect right to be on that start line. You may also be moving more comfortably and for less effort than someone shuffling along trying to run at 5mph. If you also remember that most of the field will walk most of the climbs … all you need to do is work on your climbing strength and descending skill.

In fact, if you have a look around that start line you will see all shapes and sizes, and if you ask you will get a whole range of running histories. Remember Dr Sam Robsons' 2012 study mentioned earlier?

'There appears to be no direct link between the number of years spent running, the current weekly mileage, marathon pb and the likelihood of finishing a big ultra.'

While *time on feet* over the years does appear to be important, the good news is that other non-physical stuff is *at least* as important. So those racing snakes you see on the start line? The odds are that they won't all be there at the finish.

Finally it's worth noting that all the comparisons that happen with finishing times in the shorter road races cannot meaningfully occur in trail ultras, where every race is different. The finishing times are unique to that course on that day – and different weather can have a huge impact on finishing times. This means you can't have that Monday morning

conversation comparing ultra run finish times – though let's face it, if you do have someone else at your place of work who also gets their kicks by running over fifty miles at a weekend, you are in a rare place of work!

What *this* means is that there are very few commonly accepted, universally applicable aspirational benchmarks as per a sub three-hour marathon. In other words, it becomes much more about the experience of that race than the time on the clock: it is really and truly all about you, and not about how you compare. Your mark is your mark, and only you can judge its worth.

So the bottom line is that it's OK to jump right in, because as the distance goes up, the less of a distance runner you need to be.

In Summary

- No running history? Welcome to our world
- As the race distance goes up, the less of a runner you need to be
- Forget running: think *covering the ground*
- Train to walk
- Your run history and training matter less as the race distance increases
- All shapes and sizes will be on an ultra start line: you can be there too
- The 'normal' comparisons don't apply

REVELATIONS FROM REAL RUNNERS

Lessons and Learning

Steve Webb

- Ignore 'off the shelf' marathon training schedules. You need your own tailored to your life, your job, your body
- Listen to your body, forget the personal best, and think yourself lucky you can even contemplate an ultra
- Be prepared to travel to train
- Refuelling: I always nosedive too soon. This is crucial and depends on your own needs. Ignore anything you read in magazines, it's mostly rubbish
- If you've had an illness within a month leading up to a race, don't be surprised if you under-perform. In the event, if it feels like it's going that way, just get what you can from the experience. No shame in DNF if it comes to that, and it might be the wise thing to do
- Eat well. Endurance training is not a licence to eat too much of what you want. Get some appropriate advice and stick to it

Alex Mason

Every time I run and race it's a lesson: I try to find what works, tweak it and enhance it. Lots of books and people give advice, and the best advice I've come across is that everyone is different and what works for one may not work for another. Just take the best bits and try them.

I'm lucky so far and haven't had a DNF. I've only done four ultras, and in the ultra world these have been relatively easy ones: the longest at 100K was flat as a pancake. Although tough they have been good introductions.

I think everyone's first ultra will always be the most memorable one. I've never run a marathon, and my first ultra was the High Peak 40 – it was three times the distance of my longest race, which was a half marathon, so was quite an experience.

I didn't have any expectations, just to finish. I set off at a fair pace and was wondering why people were walking on the first incline – I thought they were a bunch of wimps, so ran up the hill and passed quite a few. I even tried running up Mam Tor and Deep Dale, which I mostly did but then ground to a halt about ten miles from the end, and it took me two and a half hours to do ten miles! Anyway I finished and said '*Never again!*'

I've since done it again.

John Oldroyd

At 2.00a.m. the streets of Ambleside were dark and deserted, and the bright lights of 'The Lakes Runner' shop were shining like a beacon as I approached. The shop was the checkpoint at about mile eighty-seven in the 2009 Ultra Tour Lake District. I pushed open the door and seemed to enter a parallel universe. The shop staff, family and friends were having a party. Music was playing from a sound system, there was a guy with a bass guitar playing along, and there were two guys with a microphone belting out a duet: this was a karaoke party!

There were no other UTLD runners there, so I had their undivided attention. I was immediately made to feel like an honoured guest at their party, and encouraged to sit down and rest. I was offered a wide choice of food and drink. Nothing was too much trouble for my hosts. How about a beer? Much as I would have enjoyed a beer, I was certain that it would send me straight to sleep. Hot, sweet tea for me, please.

I was then offered the microphone! Did I have a favourite song I would like to give them? No? Well how about a request? Bruce Springsteen, 'Born to Run' perhaps? Or how about Queen, 'Don't Stop Me Now'? This was my second night without sleep, and decision-making was beyond me!

When someone found the music from 'Chariots of Fire' the shop was full of slow-motion runners. It was with this music that I was ushered back out into the night. Surreal is the only word to describe the experience; I know I was laughing all the way over Loughrigg fell. Cheers guys!

When you get to a checkpoint – smile. They really are pleased to see you. The checkpoint staff are invariably volunteers, and remember that they are also going without sleep to help you on your way. The very least you can do when you leave is to say 'Thank you'.

Annie Carrington

Success is measured in different ways by runners; for some it means speed, and for others it is to finish a race. My main criterion for success at the moment is to finish my race/event with some enjoyment – speed has taken a back seat for now. (I still find it hard to let this one go because I would really love to whip some people, but I have to let it go right now.) I have odd moments of misery and lack of enjoyment, but they are few and far between, and I do get some strange kind of pleasure from finishing a race that I have struggled with. When my event goes well it gives me greater confidence, I feel strong mentally and this transfers to my physical body, which feels strong and able to endure. I have faith in myself to finish.

I actually enjoy the act of running, not just the step-by-step act of running but the journey I am on. I love the shared moments of that journey, the fellow runners and the camaraderie. The journey can be hard, but it is a way of travelling and relying on oneself, and having the knowledge of success is a great boost. I try to remember and revisit the numerous events I have been successful in, and use this positively … I *can* do this.

In nearly thirty years of running I have had four DNFs, but a lot of races have been run in that time, and I know exactly why I didn't finish! In the first – it was too, too hot, my head was about to explode, not enough to drink. In the second – I was pregnant and didn't know, I had a complete lack of energy, I felt it drain away through the floor after four miles of fourteen! In the third – I was unprepared mentally, my head was not in the right place. And the fourth – I had races too close together: I'd had a good time in a road marathon, and then six days later ran a long fell race, which was totally unrealistic.

From this I have learnt to be prepared physically, be prepared mentally, and not to kid myself, but be realistic. It's no use thinking that what was achievable ten years ago still stands at this present time, because things change! I have learnt to try and listen to my body, to try and keep my head in a positive place, and to be realistic. Also to continually question why I am doing something, and keep to my game plan! Don't be swayed by others, and don't get involved in pre-race conversations about form and times. Be honest with myself – probably the hardest part of all.

CHAPTER 3

Ultra-running Truths

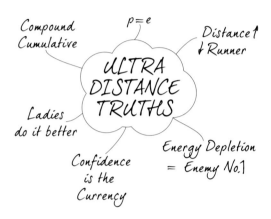

Compound
Cumulative

$p = e$

Distance↑
↓ Runner

ULTRA
DISTANCE
TRUTHS

Ladies
do it better

Confidence
is the
Currency

Energy Depletion
= Enemy No.1

Muscle Tissue Damage

The worst result of muscle tissue damage is being reduced to the 'ultra-runner shuffle' – usually seen in the final quarter of a race when good posture has gone to hell and all hope of a dignified finish has evaporated. This particularly affects the quad muscles of the upper legs – they are the largest muscle group we have – and they get trashed most on the downhill parts of the race. The chief culprit is known as DOMS: Delayed Onset of Muscle Soreness. Sport scientist Marc Laithwaite (www.endurancecoach.com) explains more:

'The term 'DOMS' is used frequently in the world of endurance. The name refers to the fact that sometimes you don't actually feel the effects of a training session or race until the following day when you step out of bed.

So what's happened? Has someone been repeatedly battering your tired legs throughout the night whilst you failed to wake from your exercise-induced, coma-like sleep? The answer lies with DOMS and the inflammation process.'

Most people slow down in the course of a race, and although there are some exceptions to this at the top of the sport, generally speaking I find that this holds true. The study by Dr Sam Robson at the 2012 South Downs Way 100 certainly found that the first quarter of the race was the fastest – especially for the men in the field (more about that later …). So the issue becomes *who slows down the least* – and the two main factors that influence this are muscle tissue damage and the 'central governor' – the fact that fatigue is controlled by the brain.

The Inflammation Process

During a long running event the muscle tissue is damaged due to repeated stress, and this triggers the inflammation process. The damage occurs during the marathon, but the inflammation process takes twenty-four to forty-eight hours to reach its peak; thus the cause of the pain you feel the following morning was actually happening 'real time' during the second half of the race.

An important note to make here is that when people slow down in the final miles of a long run, we generally assume it is caused by low carbohydrate stores – often termed *hitting the wall.* However, as we have said, there is likely to be a significant amount of muscle tissue damage by this stage in the race, and this will undoubtedly have an impact upon performance. Due to the DOMS effect, we rarely discuss the significance of tissue damage *during* the event, but as mentioned above, it's important to recognize that the pain you experience twenty-four to forty-eight hours after the race is caused by damage that happens 'real time' in the second half of the race.

How does damage affect performance? You don't have to be a rocket scientist to understand that a damaged muscle will not work as effectively as a healthy muscle. However, aside from the actual physical damage directly affecting performance, it's possible that the inflammation process is acting on a much higher plane and going straight to the governor – your brain.

The Central Governor

There are various theories on slowing down, and one of the most prominent is the 'central governor' (read Tim Noakes and Matt Fitzgerald if you want to know more). This theory suggests that fatigue is controlled by the brain, which can effectively switch off nerve signals to muscles – rather than fatigue being controlled by 'peripheral factors' such as the actual muscle damage. For example:

- The muscle is damaged and therefore doesn't work well, and as a result you slow down. That is *peripheral control*: the muscle is damaged and doesn't work, but at no point is the brain involved
- The muscle is damaged and somehow the brain's monitoring system detects this. As a result the brain blocks nerve signals to the muscle so it can't function fully and you are forced to slow down. Alternatively the brain might make you think you're exercising harder than you actually are, so as to force a reduction in your speed. That is *central governor control*, as the brain is calling the shots

Just because the brain is involved, we are not entering the realms of psychology – don't think that this can be overridden by 'mind over matter'. Your mental strength is not what we are talking about here.

Muscle Damage Limitation

Signs of Muscle Damage

- The muscle will be very tender, warm and swollen, and if someone squeezes your leg you'll instinctively want to punch them
- When you stretch, it makes no difference to the tenderness, and the pain still exists (it's not tight, it's damaged) and it's probably better if you actually don't stretch

Treatment of Muscle Damage

- Rest and let your legs recover for a few days
- Avoid post-event massage or stretching; sticking fingers into or stretching damaged tissue is never a good idea – wait a few days at least
- Eat the right foods that encourage reduced inflammation and rapid repair
- After a few days do light exercise to encourage blood flow and assist the repair process

Prevention of Muscle Damage

- Damage will be far greater if you're not conditioned to the distance and terrain. Specifics such as running downhill and running with a pack all need to be considered as part of the training mix
- It's possible that damage may be reduced by using compression clothing. Research is very poor, but subjective feedback suggests that it certainly can help
- Nutritional interventions can also help – specific foods and supplements can combat inflammation and help your recovery and performance

This is an edited extract. The full article is available at www.theendurancecoach.com

The Implications for Training and Racing

So the implication of muscle damage for our training is that we need to bombproof our legs: we need to become *skilled, strong and efficient at descending.* That's completely different from simply embracing gravity, taking the shortest line and throwing caution to the wind: preservation and conservation are the watchwords here.

Hill Homework

Hill repeats are a key feature for most running training programmes, and most of these have us running *up*hill. The benefits cited include leg strength and power – and getting better at running uphill and feeling incredibly self-righteous afterwards. Personally speaking, if someone offered me those benefits on a plate I'd take them, but if I were seeking to *really* maximize the use of my limited training time – a reality for those of us who have to work for a living – I might do it slightly differently.

Walk Up

In ultras, most people slow down on a hill, right? The difference in speed between a fast economical walk and a slow run may be very small. The difference in actual and perceived effort may, however, be considerable, and the benefits of a change in style – and in ultras a change really can be as good as a rest – are similarly considerable. All of that means that I might choose to get really good at walking up the climbs and accelerating over the top when most people are preoccupied with sucking air.

A technique for a walking climb up a steep slope: chin forward, body more upright, hands to top of knees, smaller steps.

A technique for a walking climb up a gentle slope: long stride, low body, chin up, exaggerated arm swing.

Run Down

The sure-fire way of damaging leg muscle tissue quickly and stimulating DOMS is to embrace gravity with some healthy headlong plummeting. The top British fell racers are superb at this (*see* Richard Askwith's seminal work *Feet in the Clouds*), and while the skill and style required to run fast and smooth downhill over rough terrain is in some ways very different to that required for an ultra race, the bomb-proofing effect is huge. In short: run fast down, get sore, recover, do it all again.

Make it Harder

Again, if we're working with the reality of limited time, then progressing by simply doing more and more repeats is only going to get us so far. Strapping on a loaded rucksack will up the training effect by adding more load: more load to haul uphill and more load to compensate for on the descent. However, remember the rule when introducing anything new: start small and build progressively at a rate you can cope with.

The technique for a running climb: upright posture, small steps, exaggerated elbow drive back.

Hold Posture and Form

Taking active control of your posture and running form is another way of minimizing the effect of muscle damage. If you're floating along perfectly balanced and aligned regardless of the terrain under your feet, then you're putting less stress through your tissues and that means you'll be able to preserve good function for longer. Just because running *per se* is a mechanically simple activity that we can all do without much thought doesn't mean there are not several refinements we can make so that the action becomes more efficient. Anything you can do to lighten your step is consistent with minimizing impact forces and delaying DOMS.

Here are some techniques you can adopt:

- Shorten your stride (more of this in *Feet* later)
- Check how loud your footfalls are and switch your focus to *running quietly*
- Use car/shop windows to check your posture as you run past. Are you *running tall* and symmetrical, or do you resemble some kind of demented banana on legs?
- Get yourself filmed if you have no windows …
- Find a good role model

I Know This Because ...

Running with a Role Model

Running with my friend Speedy Paul is an education. I say 'running with', but what I actually mean is running with him on the warm-up and cool-down – because when the fun starts Paul flies and I'm still very much earthbound: the clue's in his name, you see.

Anyway, in an attempt to keep the elastic from snapping completely we've learned to use handicapping – he gives me a start – and even if we hardly see each other during an interval set, we both stay a little more honest knowing that there's someone else sharing the same stretch of road at some ungodly hour of the morning. Paul's real value is that he shuts me up.

You see, Paul doesn't run like a normal earthbound soul – he glides. It's a beautiful thing to behold and he hardly makes a sound. Now I'm a significantly quieter running bloke than I was just because I've learned the link between noise and mechanical efficiency, and I've made the adjustments. But running next to Paul forces me to tune in and match his stealth mode: it's a wonderful exercise in mirroring and modelling, and for a short while at least I get to experience some of what it must be like to be Speedy Stealth Paul. Passing through the countryside with hardly a sound and a conscious effort? What's not to like!

Control Your Pace

All things being equal, the faster we run, the more impact force we experience, and this is particularly so if our running style is mechanically inefficient (clue: you know those people who run and sound as if they want to leave holes in the ground?). This means that if we blast off the start line and make the first quarter by far and away the swiftest part of our race, we've probably just done two things we'll regret later:

- Given the legs a disproportionate hammering
- Dug disproportionally deep into our energy reserves

At the 2010 Lakeland 100-mile trail race I deliberately went out in second place on course record pace for the first quarter, and then tried to hang on. I wanted to know what it felt like to run at the front – *could I do it?* – and I figured that my 'slow' might still be good enough. To this day I'll tell you that I think a flying first seventy minutes – OK, it's all relative I know – which included a plummeting 600m rocky descent, generated muscle tissue damage that I was managing from thereon in – despite the fact that I was very fit – and which the cumulative effort progressively exacerbated. I did hang on to finish second, but the second half was slow by comparison and the final quarter was very, very slow – and very, very painful.

Remember Dr Sam Robson's study mentioned at the top of this section? It's the *women* who tend to get the pace right over the first part of a race. By doing that they are preserving muscle function for longer and conserving their energy expenditure – both actions that load the dice in favour of a strong finish. Robson's study offers some explanation into why that's the case, and what women tend to do differently. Taking that and my own studies, the implications for a successful racing strategy could be this:

- Get real: ensure your pace goals match your conditioning or be ready to suffer later
- Start with the finish in mind
- Take the pressure off your pace in the first part of the race by using distraction

Using Distraction to Control Pace

As a Coach

A client came to me dissillusioned after a string of DNFs. He was a good runner with a long history and well conditioned, but he'd got himself into a pattern of not finishing, and part of the problem was that he was thinking too much about it all and getting himself into a right mess.

Objective: Put his attention somewhere else and somewhere positive.

Solution: Put him in the role of mentor and shepherd by completing – not *competing* – alongside someone slower and less experienced.

So he ran with a newbie lady in her first big ultra, distracted himself by putting his attention on her and on the process of enjoying the race, crossed a finish line for the first time in ages and therefore broke his pattern of DNFs.

As a Triathlete

In my former life I was a multi-sport bum, and my pb over Ironman distance (2.4 miles swim, 112 miles cycle, 26 miles run) came in South Africa in the mid-1990s. One of my goals was to negative-split the bike leg – ride a faster second half than the first – so I could set up for a strong run. I chose to pack a small camera in the pocket of my bike jersey and spent the first half of the bike course taking periodic pictures of the jaw-dropping scenery – I was in SA for the first time – and the other competitors. My race started after 56 biking miles, so I did ride a faster second half, and I did finish strong.

As an Ultra Runner

My best result from my three finishes at the Lakeland 100 trail race came in 2011. I'd changed my training quite a bit, so many of my usual measures of progress had been missing. The result was that I thought I was less fit – and I was certainly less confident than in previous years. Except in 2010 I'd come second, and as far as quite a few folks were concerned, 2011 was due to be my year. No pressure then.

Running buddies: two legs or four – take your pick.

I wanted to do something I'd never done before – to run a big ultra at even pace. I decided that the race for me would start at sixty miles, and that meant I had to stay in my bubble with everything in the green till then. I started right at the back of the field and walked most of the first mile. At mile sixty I was in equal second place and had arrived at that point only five minutes down on my split from 2010 – when I'd gone off like a rocket and just tried to hold on. The difference one year on was that I was in complete control and ready to rock. I went on to finish seventy minutes faster, and sixty-five of those came over the final quarter of the race.

Control Your Pace: An Alternative View

You could, of course, simply do just the opposite: run as fast as you can for as long as you can.

You already know that most people are going to slow down, so why not use your energy when you are at your freshest to cover the most ground in the fastest possible time with the least amount of effort? You may be slowing down horribly in the latter stages, but so is everyone else – and if you've got a time and distance gap as a cushion and your goal is a top place, then even if the gap closes the cushion remains.

The best advocate of this I know is UK-based Stuart Mills. Stuart will routinely set off like a rocket, and usually – though not always – that's the last you'll see of him till the finish. Stuart feeds off emotion and tries to work a

Even the most experienced ultra runners have to slow down sometimes.

very simple feedback loop while he's racing, along the lines of: '*If I'm running fast I'm feeling good, and if I'm feeling good …*'

Now Stu has been racing for decades and is a superbly conditioned athlete with a thinking head on his shoulders. No doubt his is a gutsy way to run, not least because I think it requires a hefty amount of emotional resilience to go with the mental strength required to pull it off: fine when the feedback loop is working, but once that falters the fun really begins …

You can read more about Stuart's Race-Focus-Energy-Fatigue model on www.ultrastu.blogspot.co.uk

In Summary

- The issue is, who slows down the least
- Get smart and effective about managing muscle damage and DOMS
- Slowing: a brain-induced safety mechanism?
- Inflammation is a vital part of the healing process
- Hill repeats don't just mean going *up*
- Take control of your form
- Find a running role model
- Control your ego and your early pace

Implications for Training

- Descend-proof your legs: condition the muscles and develop a smooth style
- Reduce your footprint: lighten up
- Practise pace control: use negative split sessions where the second half is faster or at least more intense

Implications for Racing

- Set pace goals consistent with your conditioning and/or your willingness to hang on
- Eat for health and repair
- Explore compression kit

Fuel Depletion is the Enemy

Fuel Depletion due to Pace

We've seen already that running 'too fast' in the first half of the race can dig disproportionately deep into our energy reserves, which we are likely to pay for later – unless we are disciplined and clear-headed enough to keep eating and drinking. All things being equal, the faster the pace, the more energy is required. Running out of energy has to be one of the worst feelings in the world, and if you're on a mission to *get somewhere* under your own steam it can seriously ruin your day. So keeping topped up by eating and drinking regularly is indeed one of the disciplines required – but that's only part of the story.

A conversation with the head of The Spine Race medical team (a seven-day winter ultra in the UK: www.thespinerace.com) before the 2014 race revealed one fundamental constant: every issue the team dealt with in the 2013 race – apart from catastrophic injuries such as falls and trips – was caused in whole or in part by runners getting the fuel thing wrong and running out of energy. A conversation about trends in relevant studies with Dr Howard Hurst, Head of Sport and Exercise Science at University of Central Lancashire, backed that up, and a third conversation with performance nutritionist Rebecca Dent (www.rebeccadent. co.uk) cemented it. My own Did Not Finish in the 2014 race was almost entirely due to this – so go back and read that first paragraph again because it's important.

Taking the glorified picnic approach can lead to stomach problems as the body's systems

– already occupied as they are with the task of relentless forward motion over an extended length of time by a highly complex being (you) – become overloaded trying to process the constant calorie influx. If our brains could speak – and mine certainly can – it might sound something like this: '*Look buddy, can't you see I've got my hands full here – and you want me to do what as well?*'

We all have an astonishing level of internal energy supplies – the issue is whether we can tap in and use them *and* continue to have the motivation to do that while maintaining forward progress in a complex, changing, challenging environment.

Losing my mind after hours in the rain.

Fuel Depletion due to Mindlessness

In other words you forget. Or you remember, but just can't be bothered. Or you remember and can be bothered, but you don't take on enough to arrest the decline.

When the weather is extreme and you're feeling sorry for yourself, can you still maintain fuel discipline in order to generate the energy to keep moving forward and stay warm?

When other things happen and your attention narrows, one of the first casualties is big-picture perspective and proactivity. 'Other things' might be:

- Bad weather
- Running (too) fast
- Death or glory ding-dong battle with a rival

The risk is made more acute if you are running solo because the only person who can register the warning signs is you – and that requires you to be self-aware enough to know what your warning signs are, and motivated enough to act on that information. That usually means *making a change*, and that's tough when it's tough – far easier to just keep doing what you're doing …

In January 2014 I made my second attempt to reach the finish line of Britain's most brutal ultra, the Spine Race (www.thespinerace.com). At around mile sixty at the start of the first night I got the first indication that there was a big problem brewing. Here's an extract from my race report:

There is, however, one thing in my world that is starting to puzzle me: every time I drink I want to pee a few minutes later. Every time. I can't believe I'm over-hydrated – I'm not exactly Sweat City here, and I didn't drink all my 1.5 litres during the first forty-five miles – but what else can it be?

It's only when I'm at checkpoint two at 105 miles and quizzing the race doctor that understanding comes. When the body is cold the brain will trigger urination to get rid of as much fluid as possible so the blood can concentrate on warming the vital organs. My frequent peeing for no apparent (thirst) reason is a *big* sign that I'm cold – and probably have been since well into the first day. Except I don't feel that cold – OK, I'm not toasty – but I'm not shivering either. It's another reason I don't register there might be a problem.

Another reason is that I've trained to operate in a depleted state, and that means the true extent of the decline is being masked. Meanwhile dehydration is working its own stealth attack …

The fixes are one, or all of these three: eat more, wear more, or work harder. Anyway, realization is for later – for now I don't have the knowledge to make the connection so I simply continue to drink (cold water – and I'll find out later this is another factor in my decline), pee, and add/remove layers as I feel – all the while continuing to dig myself into a hole that two days later I will be unable to climb out of.

More on this in Chapter 7.

Fuel Depletion due to Fuel Inefficiency

Part also lies in becoming more fuel-efficient: Think diesel versus turbo-charged petrol engine – or think *camel*: can cover huge distances without having to stop to refuel.

If you want a kitchen analogy think *fast boil to slow simmer*. It is normal to come into ultrarunning with a metabolism that relies on frequent hits of carboydrate and sugar to operate. This is, after all, what much of the Western diet is based on. This is perpetuated by some historically accepted beliefs, messages and habits in and around endurance sport, such as:

• Carbo-loading (and carbohydrate is king)
• Drink-drink-drink (your isotonic drinks)
• Three gels after every hour of exercise

These all have their place, it's just that in ultrarunning we want an engine that ticks along quite nicely thank you without all that much care and attention. And anyway – have you seen the price of fuel these days..?

For us ultra folks this means making the transition from relying on frequent ingestion of mainly sugar-based foods and a veritable food-fest at race checkpoints, to being able to exist on nothing but sucking moisture from grass. OK – slight exaggeration there, but the goal remains:

To develop a highly efficient engine that takes most of its fuel from our internal stores and can chug along quite happily for many miles between services.

I Know This Because ...

I was first introduced to fuel efficiency in my triathlon days back in the 1990s by my coach at that time who was helping me prepare for Ironman distance. It became quite normal to go into the second session of the day at least four hours after the first with nothing but orange juice to consume between sessions. I remember thinking that this was seriously revolutionary at the time, and it did take a real effort to lay off the calorie replenishment.

Here's how I did it when I focused on becoming a more fuel-efficient runner over the winter of 2008–9:

- Gave myself a six-month window
- Chose specific outings, during which I deliberately and progressively limited what I ate and drank
- Continued to pack full supplies for these outings just in case
- Kept the pace *slower than normal* and steady during these outings – walking is perfectly acceptable and probably essential early on
- Start with a 1½ to 2hr outing and build progressively
- Gave myself permission to feel crap

By the end of that winter I could be out on my feet for five to six hours and function on less than 500ml of water. It took me a long time to build up, and I blew up horribly on a number of early trips as I was just moving too fast and using too much energy. As someone once said to me, 'It's OK to feel like s*** in training …' and certainly I do recall some less than happy-smiley moments in the early days of this process. Once I was brave enough to slow right down I was OK.

I continue to reap the benefits of that transformation, a recent and vivid example being during a race on the Pennine Way long-distance footpath in January 2013 (so that's in the depths of the English winter, dark, cold and generally inhospitable). I stopped for a pee at about ninety miles after being on the move for nearly thirty hours, and some urine landed on my bare leg. My ph balance was so shot the urine burnt my skin enough to make me yell in shock – and yet I was still moving along pretty well and still thinking clearly. Despite being very dehydrated I was still able to operate – which I attribute to my depletion sessions, which accelerated the process of becoming a much more fuel-efficient runner than I was when I started ultra running in 2003.

The good news is that it is perfectly possible to train to become more fuel-efficient: it takes a while and it can be humbling in the first few weeks – but it's perfectly possible. The method I have explored is fasting or depletion workouts: progressively limiting what I eat and drink in order to train my fuel system to operate (for longer) on less.

Fuel Efficiency: Why Bother?

- Less food and drink to carry
- Smaller bag to carry less food and drink
- Feel lighter because of the points above
- Feel faster/easier because of the point above
- Can operate on less, and have simpler foods and drink – easier on the body
- Eat and drink less/less often – less time spent at checkpoints
- Confidence: you know you'll be OK if you miss a feed
- It's just cheaper

In Summary

- Energy depletion: is this at the heart of every poor performance and DNF?
- Energy depletion is due to fast pace, mindlessness, inefficient engine
- Running fast requires more energy – so up the intake
- Keep it simple: beware overloading a system that is already working hard
- Our internal energy supplies are plenty – the challenge is to tap in and use them
- Stay on task as the stakes get higher: preserve mindfulness
- Warning: proactivity goes out the window when our attention narrows to 'other stuff'
- The clues are all around us if we have the wit and knowledge to register them
- Become like a camel – train to go a long way on very little

Winter ultras bring their own special challenges: five miles gone and 263 to go for runners in the 2014 Spine Race. (SUMMIT FEVER PHOTOGRAPHY)

REVELATIONS FROM REAL RUNNERS

Bad Weather and Mindlessness

Ray Wheatley

Ultra running plays tricks on the mind, especially when you are at a physical or mental low point. I've experienced two DNFs caused by ignorance and misjudgement, and the physical stresses and mental challenges experienced are not to be taken lightly, as I found out to my cost.

My second attempt at the Hardmoors 55 in 2012 saw me start with lighter kit and reduced weight from the first year, a lighter, proper running pack to carry all my kit in, and bottles instead of a three-litre bladder. What an improvement: it all felt better, and I was running freely until Carlton Bank, where it started to rain heavily. This is where mental misjudgement occurred. I knew I needed to put on my waterproofs, but I kept putting it off, thinking the rain would ease. But it got heavier, and the higher I climbed, the wetter and colder it got. I told myself I'd stop at the top of the hill where I knew there was a seat to sit on where I could put on my leggings. At the top of the climb I finally put on my waterproofs over my wet clothes – but this was a bad mistake, because being cold and wet, when I tried to generate heat by running to keep warm my body didn't want to share the energy with my legs, so I ended up walking and getting colder. The result was, when I arrived at the next indoor checkpoint I had developed mild hypothermia, forcing me to DNF.

Lesson: heed the signs.

Simon Bright

In 2012 I went through my first of two DNFs. I never expected this to happen to me, I believed I was tough enough to keep going, but I ended up a blubbering mess and decided I was an abject failure for giving in. Not a good experience, but something that taught me to focus on what I had achieved, rather than my apparent lack of success. And one of the things these DNFs helped me achieve was a better understanding of the demands of ultra running.

First, it made me recognize that sometimes stopping isn't the easiest option, but the only option. With hindsight I realized I was probably in the early stages of hypothermia and could have been in serious trouble if I'd carried on (a message that was driven home when I found out a few months later that an ultra runner had died on another race due to hypothermia-induced heart failure).

You Can Sleep on the Job

Rules About Sleep

The second thing I learned was to respect the environment we run in, and to take it seriously. It can be as harsh as it is beautiful, and it isn't possible to ignore the challenges it presents with impunity. These challenges can include things we would find trivial in other circumstances, such as rain and cold, but they can have a disastrous impact in ultras.

Just as importantly, I learned to respect and listen to my own body. Basically it was making me stop – not because of a lack of moral fibre or whatever, but because it was in trouble and I needed to get somewhere where it was safe.

It is perfectly OK to grab some shut-eye time during a race, and for those events where you go through a day and a night and into the following day you may find yourself losing out in the battle of drooping eyelids anyway. If you're on the go for that length of time, then ten, twenty, forty, sixty minutes' sleep is really neither here nor there, and may be the difference which makes the difference in the end. If you do choose to take the sleep option then here are two rules:

- Always sleep at an aid station*– other people out walking or running tend not to appreciate finding an unexplained body at the side of the path
- Always tell the people in charge of the aid station that you will be sleeping – those people don't appreciate tripping over an unexplained body in their jurisdiction either

*   If you are racing to win, then from a tactical perspective this might not be such a good idea because what happens in the aid station absolutely does not stay within its bounds – aid stations are a hotbed of news and activity. If you want to keep your competition guessing, then keeping your problems/choices to yourself (and your crew) is key. Aid station volunteers are sources of information for the runners coming in, and the last thing you want to do is give your chasing competition reasons to feel optimistic. So 'she was here for twenty minutes, had to fix some blisters, had a sleep for ten minutes and walked out of here complaining of cramp' is the news equivalent to a banned substance for your pursuers.

If you know it's going to be a longer than a planned stop with a nap, then it's better to get through the aid station quickly whilst giving the impression of maximum perkiness, and then stop and sort yourself out some way beyond it and out of sight. If you have a support crew this could be something arranged in advance or that you handle 'on the fly'. The general rule as far as your competition is concerned is 'hope suppression' – so keep 'em guessing, because in ultras if you're out of sight you really are out of mind.

How Long Should I Sleep?

That depends on factors such as …

- How long the event is
- Previous 'on the job' sleep experience
- Your event goals
- How close you are to cut-off times
- How self-reliant you are
- How busy the aid station is/how much sleep space is available
- How you feel
- What kit you have available
- What you believe you will gain or lose

As for the duration itself, my own experience is that a recharge of sorts can be gained by sitting for as little as half a minute with the eyes closed. I remember doing just this at the ninety-five point of a 100-mile race, asking the marshall to prod me after thirty seconds: the first time I'd sat down all race and it just helped me gather myself for the final bit.

Dr Mike Stroud in his book *Survival of the Fittest* (2004) has collected together considerable data on this as part of his polar exploration projects with our greatest living explorer Ranulph Fiennes. He presents a case for a forty-five-minute sleep window:

- I don't know what a definitive answer is, even if there is one. It depends …
- I do think it's a function of confidence, and it's probably less than you think you need or what the physiological theory says
- Remember *performance is emotional*, so if you *feel* better, you'll move better – whether that's off a ten- or a 100-minute recharge

Multi-day adventure racers go for a week on what appears to be ridiculously small amounts of sleep – and while it's undoubtedly easier with team-mates around you and with a change of discipline to look forward to, the fact remains that they do operate on what most of us would regard as very little shut-eye time. I do think it's harder when you are solo and are purely on a weight-bearing mode of travel, and therefore all things being equal the sleep requirement will be greater. What that might be for you and your event depends …

So what's possible? If we go back to the Spine Race of January 2014, Czech Pavel Paloncy set a new record time for the 268 winter miles at just under five days. His total sleep time? Five hours.

How Should I Sleep?

I'm not about to prescribe a specific body position here, and you will see runners at checkpoints sleeping sitting, lying, clothed or … Again, it depends on the above, and within that I'd offer these suggestions:

Get your Legs up

This stops the blood pooling in the lower legs and thereby makes it easier to get going again. So either sit with your feet propped up opposite you, or lie down with your feet elevated higher than your heart.

Plug your Ears

If you have any hopes of getting any meaningful shut-eye in a busy checkpoint, even if there is a separate sleep area, then ear plugs are invaluable. A sleep mask or similar for your eyes will complete your look.

In Summary

- It's OK to take a sleep break
- Do it at a checkpoint and do let a marshall know
- If you are racing to win or for a high place, remember that checkpoints leak: what goes on in the CP will not stay in the CP
- How long to sleep for? That depends – but probably less than you think
- Get your feet up and plug your ears

Personal Organization

Personal organization is otherwise known as reducing the faff factor, since simple (and important) tasks are made immeasurably more complicated by sloppy personal organization. Consider the following scenarios:

- Your blister repair kit is right at the bottom of your bag
- You can't reach your drink bottle without taking your backpack off
- Your route map deteriorates in bad weather because you haven't packed a plastic cover

This then requires you to spend a disproportionate amount of time and effort solving the problem, which you resent because it distracts you from the task of relentless forward motion and forces you to face up to your mistake. Which makes you feel awful. And if you feel awful you tend to focus on stuff which makes you feel even worse – and potentially that's the end of the road for you because *performance*

... Or ignore it, or try to sort it, then give up because it's a faff ...

is emotional. You need to snap out of it, except *that* requires a strategy and *that* requires you've thought about it in advance. So it's easier not to bother – and wallow. Oh dear.

Think about it this way: if you were planning to cycle round the world there are three good reasons why you'd do it on a steel frame machine without suspension and as few gears as you can get away with. Because?

- Such a machine is lighter and more robust
- There are fewer bits to break
- When something does go wrong you can probably fix it

So it is with the ultra-marathon runner and their kit: simple, effective, bombproof and retrievable works every single time.

Personal Equipment

Strapped, Wrapped and Accessible
I've seen shirts shredded, and backs, shoulders and hips rubbed raw because of a poorly fitted and adjusted rucksack or bumbag. This problem is reducing with the rising popularity of profile-hugging race vests, but the fact remains that if it's a sloppy fit, poorly packed or you can't easily access zips and pockets with one hand/in the dark/in bad weather/when you're bushed, then there'll be tears later.

Pimp my Pack
You can increase the carrying options considerably by adding you own bungee cords and elastic sleeves – and if you're less than a dab hand with a sewing machine, then your local works/school uniform supplier or independent outdoor or sailing kit supplier may help. Elastic sleeves can be sewn into shoulder, hip or chest straps, while bungees can be threaded across the front and sides of your pack. There's a lot to be said for your own custom job.

Eating and Drinking

Can You Drink on the Move?
Bladders are great for this, but some types are easier to fill and secure back in your pack than others – and unless you suck the air out of the top of a partly full bladder, the sloshing sound can drive you nuts.

Pimp my pack: bungee cord across the front; elastic sleeves added to shoulder straps; additional pouch threaded to your waistbelt.

Can you Reach your Bottles?

Again, this problem is reducing as more and more running packs add user-friendly angled side and front pockets – but if you can't get at and replace a bottle easily one-handed on the move, you will be inclined not to bother later.

Where are Your Favourite Nibbles?

Somewhere easy to reach one-handed, I hope, and you may also have partly opened those wrappings you have learned are less than straightforward when you have slick fingers and are two-thirds into the race.

Where will You Put your Litter?

Despite all the environmental impact messages we now have around us, most races still have their share of litter louts. Some events, such as Ultra Tour Mont Blanc in France, are proactive to the point of issuing personal nylon litter bags to all runners, while other events have just stopped using plastic cups at checkpoints altogether. A plastic bag tucked into a waist/pocket or similar that is emptied at checkpoints is all you need – and you do need it. I know of occasions in the UK when races have not happened in a following year because the landowner has refused permission after runners have littered and defecated along the route seemingly without a care to the consequences of their selfish, thoughtless actions.

Navigation

It is important to make navigation user friendly:

If you prefer working from written instructions and the organizer gives you a map – you're in trouble.

If you have to squint at the font size or detail in the calmness of your own home, then you'll be in trouble later in the race.

If your map is the size of a tablecloth then you're also heading for problems.

In my experience as a coach many of the problems people have with navigation can be solved or at least greatly reduced before they even get out of the door by doing some or all of the following to reduce the faff factor:

- Choose in advance to take responsibility for the route finding
- Translate the given information into a format and size that is 'you friendly'
- Make your own route cards
- Weatherproof your route info by laminating or using plastic covers – even if the said info is purported to be on 'waterproof' paper
- Keep your route info accessible when it is not in use by either carrying it in a front sleeve or pouch, stuffing it down your top, or hanging it round your neck
- Fold your map in advance, and run with your thumb on your location when your route info is in use
- Use annotation and colour highlighting of key features
- Securing your route info to you/your kit by lanyard if the weather is bad
- Use a small magnifying glass and a head torch with variable brightness if you struggle to see detail in bad weather/at night

A Word on Phones and Faffing

We are in an age of social media, texting and 'selfies', and it is becoming normal to see runners bent over phones pre-, mid- and post-race. We can now record and share our journey easily and instantly and receive messages from folks that can pick us up when we are down.

All of that is lovely.

The flip side is that it's also a distraction, which may cause us to miss something essential – a route turning, that growing feeling of emptiness inside, that big rock sticking out over there – or be influenced by a message that we receive that causes us to make a decision we would not have otherwise made. Like, to stop.

We will all choose what's important to us: I just know folks who have learned the hard way and now carry the simplest and cheapest phone they can find pre-loaded with emergency numbers only, and which goes into the bottom of their pack. I also know people who want to practise the skills of using their senses to enjoy and record their experience … but that's just so old school, right?

In Summary

- Simplicity wins every time: effort is a drain on a precious and finite resource, namely energy
- Pay attention to the packing and securing of personal kit
- A little custom job on your pack can be transformational
- Pack your picnic for fuelling on the fly
- Pack away your litter
- Take responsibility for your route-finding before you get out on the route
- Phones: a help and a hindrance …

REVELATIONS FROM REAL RUNNERS

Weight of the World

Ray Wheatley

My first proper ultra was the Hardmoors 55 in 2011, and following some intensive reading about the previous year's event in extreme weather, I opted to be cautious and carry extra kit in case the conditions repeated themselves.

Now there is a difference between carrying extra kit which you may need, and carrying excess weight. I did both. My pack was a 25-litre walking pack into which I stuffed everything imaginable. This was a fifty-five-mile run along the Cleveland Way in North Yorkshire with checkpoints and feeding stations regularly spaced, not the Marathon de Sables in the hot desert where you carry everything to survive for days. I was advised by seasoned ultra runners at the start to try and offload some of my excess baggage, but there was nowhere to transfer it to as my finish bag was fully stuffed too. Setting off with this monster pack I slowly covered the nine miles to the first checkpoint, then persevered onward and upwards to the second checkpoint at twenty-two miles, where I ground to a halt two minutes from cut-off time totally exhausted.

Lesson: lighten up.

Mandatory Kit Lists: It's not a Faff

Simon Bright

It took two DNFs to realize that I could have avoided problems coping with bad weather if

'Big mountains attract big weather', someone once said to me. Mandatory kit lists are designed with this in mind. It all looks lovely now …

I'd regarded the mandatory kit lists for ultras as an asset, not a burden. My attitude has gone from 'Do I really need this?' to 'Am I sure I know how to make best use of this if I need to?' For example, if the mandatory kit list requires full waterproofs I make sure I've done at least one short run wearing them, so I know they will be usable if necessary in a race.

These lessons all seem to be about what I did wrong. But the most important thing I took away was to value what I achieved and put this in perspective. Okay, I failed to complete the run, but what I can take away is that even failure was completing thirty-five miles, which is more than most people could dream of doing.

Similarly my screensaver on my computer is from my second DNF – the North Face CCC – showing the climb up to Col de Ferret. I didn't complete the run, but did complete this section in very hard conditions, which is something I take pride in. With this as a benchmark for what I achieved without feeling I'd been able to give my best, I feel a lot more confident about stepping up to other challenges strengthened by the lessons I've learnt.

Women Do It Better

I've been going on for a while now that it seemed to me, through my own coaching, racing and general curiosity around the subject, that women have got ultra marathon sorted better than blokes. They are:

- More likely to get their pacing right
- More likely to stop and sort out niggles before they become problems
- More likely to enter an ultra only after careful consideration and training

A higher proportion of women starting a race will finish as compared to men.

Throw in a propensity to leave their ego at the start line, and what we have is a higher proportion of women starting a race who will tend to finish when compared to us blokes, while at the top end of the sport the leading women are quite happy to take records outright for their own and tickle the heels of the leading men.

Is There a Typical Ultra Running Type?

No – and yes. A wide variety of physical shapes, sizes and running backgrounds were on that start line, but the common factor was mental: all runners in the sample were motivated by challenge.

Women are better at pacing themselves for the long haul.

In Summary

- Women – this is the sport for you!
- A higher proportion of women will finish than men
- Women tend to get their pacing right
- Women tend to stand on a start line well prepared
- Women are more likely to heed warning signs mid-race
- Men – learn from women!

CHAPTER 4

Getting to the Start Line

Starting Injury Free

As more and more people take up the challenge of running longer off road, the waiting lists for the big races are expanding. Why should you bother to add your name to an already big list? Because a hefty proportion of those entered will fall sick or injured in the build-up, and not even get a sniff of the start line.

A study by the Western States Research Group on the exercise behaviour of ultra runners (M.D. Hoffman, E. Krishnan, 2013) found injury to be the most significant reason why runners stopped regular running and racing (therefore not lack of time, or family pressures or falling out of love of the sport). Injury was also significant in Did Not Start rates and 'carrying' an injury also figured in Did Not Finish rates.

As the race distance goes up, the challenge of being really ready becomes an increasingly precarious balancing act – especially if you're a normal mortal who has to work for a living/ look out for a family and runs out of free choice.

That's most of us then.

Breakdown by Stealth

In comparison to road and track running, the stress on the musculoskeletal system is far less. Softer and more variable terrain underfoot reduces the impact and spreads repetitive forces (J. Uhan, 2013). This is not to say that these are not a factor – I've already argued that ultras can be described as 'repetitive strain injury writ large' – simply that by comparison to road and track they appear less and different. In addition, the generally lower level of effort means that it can all feel pretty comfortable, thank you very much.

Writing about overtraining syndrome in 2013, physical therapist and US ultra runner Joe Uhan argues that one of the unique challenges in training for trail ultras is that even after running for many hours it is entirely possible to wake up the next day feeling hardly any soreness, and conclude that the body wasn't and isn't under any stress. Not necessarily – and this is where the 'stealth' comes in.

According to Uhan, our neurological and endocrine systems are still put under pressure regardless of intensity – yet our ability to perceive stress at this level is poor. To put it another way, on the one hand the nervous system (brain and sensory organs) is 'on task' for an extended period of time managing the function of a complex organism – that's you – in a changing, challenging environment. One the other hand the endocrine system (that clever box of tricks that controls our hormones – chemical messages that carry the work instructions to the body via the blood) is also working overtime.

Public Enemy No. 1 as far as hormones are concerned is cortisol, which is released during times of physical and psychological stress – even when that stress level is relatively light. If it hangs around in the body it slows down recovery, and over time, compound and cumulative act to exacerbate the decline. And generally speaking this all happens gradually under our radar until we feel awful enough to take notice.

We make the problem worse by having the gall to actually enjoy running long on the trails. So we do more of it. People are drawn to the sport to explore and enjoy the landscape: I've never come across anyone who runs on the road for the joy of the scenery and fun of the tarmac – well, have you? – and yet 'fun of the trail' is exactly what draws many people into trail ultras. Throw in the challenge (and stress) of big climbs and descents, extreme weather and night-time all just add to the sense of adventure: 'It just don't feel like a chore …' Another reason why the early signs of deterioration can go unnoticed.

Health Then Fitness

The trick, I believe, is to strive to be healthy first and fit second. We all know people who are fit as butcher's dogs but fundamentally unhealthy – and that, my friend, is not the model we're after here. Health will give us reserves to draw on that we need during the race – especially over the very long distances – and more importantly after the race so we can recover quickly and do it all again with a smile.

Cold-water leg bath (winter version), with a good book and a mug of tea as a distraction.

Aids to Recovery

I'm going to assume that you have at least a passing acquaintance with the usual ways to aid recovery after a hard session or a race – and just to be clear, I'm talking about the following:

- A progressive cool-down – that is, not stopping dead outside your door with heart pounding and legs screaming
- Shower and change
- Drink of milk and water (a hot drink if the weather is cold)
- Cold leg bath for 3–10 minutes (then a warm shower if contrast bathing)
- Compression wear
- Lie down with the legs up
- Snack within 30 minutes
- Self massage
- Ice-cube self-massage
- Stretches
- Cycle spinning 10–30 minutes (turbo, gym or road)
- Cryotherapy (whole body freezer treatment for the very wealthy/totally sponsored)

Cold-water leg bath (summer post-race version).

For myself and the folks I work with, we've gone through a pick-and-mix process to find those that really do the job and fit into our priorities/lifestyle.

In my experience I can tell you that everything on the list above has a place when trying to stay injury free as you are beefing up the miles – but I'm not going to go into detail about them because I don't believe that *on their own* they are the habits and activities that make the biggest difference. Neither am I going to go into detail about food choices and sleep patterns here – though they, too, have a role to play.

And finally, I am *not* going to cover emotional stress, either (which is completely different to the physical stress needed as part of a progressive training plan if we are to have any hope of improving). Suffice to say that if there's a bunch of tough stuff going on in one part of your life, then unless you're world class at doing compartmentalization or you are made of stone, you can expect leakage into another part of your life. Believe me, I know.

Whether that's workplace or lifestyle in origin matters not a jot: if we're focused on something we can't control, or part of our life is out of alignment/we're adjusting to a big change for any period of time, then because we are one physical-mental-emotional unit, the symptoms may well manifest themselves in our running. That could be something specific such as sore quads or just feeling as if we're running through treacle.

In Summary

In a nutshell, do the post-run stuff, nail the food choices, get enough rest and sort your life out. Or, if you want to approach it from the other end: run lots of easy miles in locations that inspire you, and you'll find that everything else slots into place behind that.

Transform Your Training

Back-to-Back Training

Instead of a three-hour single outing, make that 2 × 1½ hours, or 2 + 1 hours spread either end of the same day, or the evening and morning of two consecutive days. There are three main advantages to this:

- It can be easier to fit in
- It is less physically stressful
- It develops mental strength as you have to get yourself out of the door a second time*

* *Great for ultras where a race is checkpoint to checkpoint, and lingering in relative comfort is a real temptation.*

Races as Training

One of the things I noticed with hindsight was that as I reached my forties I struggled to cope with combining racing the short runs while preparing for the longer ones. I guess it's obvious on one level, in that shorter and faster is higher impact, and therefore the risk of breakdown is greater. I was getting the same soft tissue problems in my calves – little muscles that do a huge amount of work – but it was only later looking back in my diary that the patterns emerged. I love to race, and moderation can be a fleeting state even today – but the result was that I was compromising training consistency, which was a problem because consistency is a key component of confidence. And in ultras, as we all know, confidence *is* the currency.

Over the last few years I've become increasingly comfortable with the idea of using medium distance races to test kit, strategy and tactics, and/or to complete them at less than 100 per cent effort and/or to use them as part of a back-to-back training block. It's a more measured approach that is less physically and mentally stressful, and all the outcomes are positive because the whole thing is just framed as one big learning and building exercise.

Know Thyself
Knowing yourself means that one runner's road to performance longevity is just that: one runner's. We all need to find what works for us and what we can handle, particularly as it would appear that the normal rules don't apply as the race distance goes up beyond the marathon. There is a great deal of consensus about how to prepare for, and race, distances up to marathon, but beyond that – and certainly getting towards 100 miles – the curious among us are still figuring it out, and what science there is, is often inconclusive.

The only way to really know is therefore to be cool with experimenting – which means that periodic disappointments are simply learning opportunities – to pay close attention to the results you get, and to keep track of it all in a diary. Over time you will see patterns and trends in the evidence you record that will help you figure out your unique success formula for consistently high personal performance.

Remember: If you are sufficiently motivated and practise the skills of perseverance and learning, you will always achieve what you want – it just might not be on your first choice timescale.

Colour Code your Training Sessions

Otherwise known as 'traffic lights', I have US ultra runner and coach Ian Torrence to thank for this one, which has transformed my ability and motivation to monitor at a glance what is happening in my world and my running. Torrence gets his runners to colour code their training sessions as recorded in their diaries:

- **Red:** fail, session aborted, cut short/ changed
- Yellow: going through the motions, nothing special
- **Green:** flying, objective achieved

The first time I used this looking back over a six-week period I was appalled to record equal proportions of red-yellow-green. In other words, only one third of what I was doing was hitting the spot. *That* got my attention …

Work–Life Balance

> You can't fire a cannon from a canoe.

I'm almost certain this is a Paul Dickenson quote (TV sport commentator and once quite a mean hammer and discus thrower, I believe), and is a favourite in the strength and conditioning world as a direct explanation as to why we should bother with strengthening the torso before any of the other fancy stuff. Or to put it another way, it's very difficult to race well over ultra distance if (bits of) the rest of your life is a bit wobbly. At least that's my experience.

It's a context and an energy thing, in that very little that happens to us does so in isolation, and I also think we have a finite supply of energy beans to use for living, working, training, loving, sharing, stretching, railing at the world, fighting – and making up. Dominoes, beans, spinning plates … you get the idea.

I Know This Because …

I'd planned a summer free from ultras in 2012 as far back as autumn 2011 – not least because the previous four summers had revolved around Daddy running 100 miles – but that all got forgotten pre-Highland Fling race in April 2012 on the back of a couple of breakthrough training weeks which had me all giddy and excited. Cue selfish Daddy and late rash entries to some summer ultras. But then the Fling flopped as I crawled from mile twenty, and pulled out twenty miles further on, and gradually over the subsequent weeks a pattern emerged.

It took me a while to admit that I'd short-changed my preparation – well, there was a huge ego to wrestle out of the way first – and had tried to bluff it without doing the work. Gradually I saw that I'd focused on the marginal gains and the smaller feel-good details while losing sight of the big picture: there were a lot of other issues I was wrestling with, and I'd simply not put the work in.

Training is physical, racing is emotional – and we can take or leave those any time we like.

That work-life-family thing, on the other hand, is a daily work-in-progress, and no note to teacher from your mum will excuse you from class.

If the currency beyond the start line is confidence, then the currency to the start line is – at least in part – stability: routine, repetition, progression, certainty. So I went all fundamentalist during summer 2012 – cleared the decks and started to race again over the shorter fell races, doing little else between start lines except periodically chase my training buddy and ride my bike. I cared not a jot for the position and time I achieved, but I relished the competitive wrestle with the other folks and with myself. It was a journey *and* a process thing; it was a much reduced time commitment, it was social not solo, and it was also back to things I could control.

Balance and Balanced

A successful work–life–running balance does not necessarily mean that you have everything in balance. You could, of course, be working like a demon from early till late, which on the face of it is a recipe for burnout. Yet if you love what you do and are clear why you are doing it … the chances are it won't feel like a chore at all. '*Stress …*' as someone else once said, '*is not being who you want to be.*'

Starting with Confidence

A starting point for this practice can be how you use your training diary. (What do you mean, you don't keep a diary?!) Your diary is your key to revealing your own formula for success – and in a sport where the normal rules don't seem to apply, and the great and the good are still searching for consensus around some key topics, your diary is your way of creating certainty – and therefore confidence – out of uncertainty. To paraphrase a certain Sir Clive Woodward during his time as coach for England rugby: '*Success, yes – but not by chance: we want to know why so we can plan for it again.*'

So analyse that good training session or race you had:

- Why did that happen?
- What was it based on?
- What factors coincided to make it so?

What you were doing in the days preceding it, who you were with, how you ate and slept, what you were thinking about, what else was happening in your life … all of these will have influenced that result – and if you recorded them in your diary the evidence will be there in black and white, and patterns and trends will be revealed over time. As long as you have the wit to see them.

Your confidence bubble can be further inflated if you choose to write about *good stuff*. At a very simple level it really does feel good to read about good stuff – especially if it's *yours*. And if you feel good you are more likely to make more good stuff happen. (Don't worry, I'm not going to go all quantum physics on you – though it is a fascinating subject … for another book.) A simple recording template for your diary consistent with this 'feel good' factor can look like this:

- What went well
- What you enjoyed
- What you learned

Focus on What You Can Control

We've already seen that as the race distances increase, harnessing your emotions to good effect becomes an even more important factor, so drip-feeding the confidence bubble is crucial. You can do this by choosing to use self-to-self comparisons – in other words, you make it completely about *you* so that when you talk to yourself – *and you do talk to yourself, right?* – you are talking yourself *towards* the finish line and not spiralling to doubts, screaming, crying, and ultimately throwing in the towel.

This is not to say that feeding off your competitors is a route to disaster – it can be highly motivating. We've all been gripped by epic ding-dong battles at the sharp end of the field where it appears that the protagonists are trying to kill each other in order to reach the finish line first. It's just that these specimins are already starting from incredibly high levels of self-belief born out of race performances and training regimes that the more ordinary of us can barely comprehend. Putting their focus on beating the other guy may well elevate their performance as long as they have the capacity and tactical acumen to match their desire. The flip side is that they are ceding control by allowing someone else to dictate their actions.

The things you can control, and which put you in a position of powerfulness, are these:

- How far *you* have come
- How good *you* are feeling
- How smartly *you* have prepared

Confidence is indeed the currency – but you need to take action to constantly replenish your reserves.

REVELATIONS FROM REAL RUNNERS

Confidence is the Currency

Simon Bright

There seem to be at least three people whenever I go running – my body, my mind and something else that isn't quite either (say, spirit/soul?). All these contribute to running, and all of them need to have their confidence built up. The obvious focus is the body – taking it out on long sessions to get it used to moving for long lengths of time (although seldom very fast in my case) and until it feels confident about doing this.

Ultras seem to need a better understanding of the importance of the mind than other types of race, including breaking down the challenge of the run into mentally digestible sections that are within your ability to comprehend. For example, on my first forty-mile training run, where I could have been overwhelmed by the distances involved, I compared the amount of mileage left to distances I knew I could complete – for example, I've done fourteen miles, so that only leaves a marathon and I know I can do those, I've done twenty-seven miles, so that only leaves a half marathon …

To help the mind break down the challenges of a run, it may be helpful to gradually increase the length of the runs, and to have already done something that was less, but nearly as, difficult, as the run you are planning to do. This might involve doing progressively longer races in the build-up to a run at a new distance (for example, working up to my first trail ultra, I progressively worked through a hard off-road half marathon, a twenty miler and a full marathon – knowing that each one was only slightly tougher than the last).

The third element – which I'll call spirit simply for want of a better name – is harder to define, and how it contributes to confidence is even trickier to explain. What I've found helpful at the start of an ultra is to have a 'justification' about why I am here. For example, I've put in all the preparation, therefore I deserve to be doing this run, and deserve to finish. When I've wanted to give up, this justification has become almost a 'mantra' to repeat and keep at bay the emotions that are threatening to undermine me.

Thinking about running as involving three persons is another strength, because if you feel one of the areas isn't strong, you can focus on reinforcing the others. If physically you are not in ideal form, invest more time in getting the mental preparation right. Not convinced you 'deserve' to do this race? Make sure you have the miles on your feet to convince yourself you are ready.

The key point about all of the above is that ultras, more than other races, may be about the completeness of the person. The pressures they put on runners can hit at any level, so all parts of the personality that make up the runner need to be strengthened and confident they can cope.

The Implications for Us All

I'll leave it to Joe Uhan to sign off this section. While I've paraphrased some of what he advocates, I've retained the key pieces of his commentary:

- Finite physical capacity: will you spread that over a lifetime, or blow it in the course of a few intense years?
- Everything happens in context: recognize that poor running performance may simply be a symptom of what is happening else-where in your life
- High volume, year-round training is unsustainable: even if the intensity level is low, don't kid yourself. Planned breaks/different activities are just as important
- Limit the number of big hard races – though it is difficult to judge how many that may be (Uhan suggests it is one to three per year)
- Lag time is real: you may not experience the hard consequences of your training and racing regime until two to three years down the line. Remember the symptoms take time to build, and will do so under your radar. Stress imbalance has roots that can extend for years
- Élite runners training and racing unsustainably are bad role models: in the absence of consistent consensus around training practices, and with much of the science inconclusive, it is entirely normal that attention is drawn to what the high profile runners are doing. Social media makes this easy, and for many people a 'quick fix' route to success will be to model what the élite do
- Take note: no matter who you are or how fast you are, these rules apply to you

In Summary

- Race full? No worries – get on the waiting list because a lot of runners will get injured before the start
- Be on the start line healthy and injury-free first – running fitness comes second
- Carrying an injury into an ultra is more likely to result in a DNF
- The usual post-race/big session recovery techniques all have a place
- Use back-to-back training if time is tight and you want to test your resolve
- Use some races as training to test strategies, add leverage and reduce the impact
- You really do need to be the expert on you
- Use colour-coding to track the quality of your training
- Your running happens in the context of all the other aspects of your life: a problem with your running may just be a symptom of a problem somewhere else
- You can be out of balance – as long as you love it
- Stick to the rules: they apply to you no matter who you are or how fast you run

REVELATIONS FROM REAL RUNNERS

Work–Life–Running Balance

Victoria Leckie

As most runners will testify, the question of balance is a precarious one for the type A personalities amongst us. I mean, the very nature of our sport means that we need to spend a long time running, and whilst some say we can always make time for what we want to in life, the reality is that we only have twenty-four hours in a day, and sacrifices will always have to be made.

So ask yourself, what are you willing to sacrifice? What compromises are you prepared to make? What are the gains and losses to be had?

When it comes to work, I'm very fortunate in that I've created a career as a freelance writer and can easily adapt my schedule to fit in with my running and other adventures. But I also have no dependents. Those with family to support are better off with the stability of a fixed income. Freelancing can be stressful! As for those with 'proper' jobs, I guess it's important to define your personal boundaries in terms of commitment to the job, and then stick with them diligently. No one ever dies wishing they'd spent more time at their desk.

Remember, too, that the happier and more well rounded an individual you are, the better your performance in the workplace will be – full stop. More important to the balance issue are the people in our lives. We all need to work out how *not* to neglect those who are important to us before it's too late. I remember having a very sobering moment during a race once when I realized that despite being just a matter of miles from my mum, whom I see seldom as we live in different countries, I was out running in a race. And for what purpose? What was I trying to prove? On the day in question, I stopped at the next aid station, hitched a lift to the nearest train station, then spent the rest of the day lunching, shopping and enjoying a wonderful time with her. It was my first and only ever DNF, but who cares? I know it's a day she'll always remember.

You see, long after our knees are knackered and our limbs are lame, it's the special times and the special people we've created them with that matter. David Allen said, 'You can do anything but not everything.' There's no destination … it requires ongoing and consistent effort. Take your eye off the ball and you'll drop it …

Ashley Charlwood

My family (wife, two daughters, animals) is important to me. The job I do (working for a not-for-profit organization) is also important – I wouldn't class myself as a wage slave. Finding a balance with the running is always hard, especially in the periods of training when it is essential to get in lots of miles. Taper and recovery is easier, and some recovery I do with my eldest daughter (aged eight) – but that's not without its issues, either.

During the lighter months, I really enjoy running early in the morning, and so that is when I tend to get out for three-hour-plus runs. This means that I can be home in time for my second breakfast with the family. The darker months, I spend a lot of time with a head torch, but 5AM starts aren't as appealing. So I tend to run *to* things. Where I live in North Wales, the nearest swimming pool is 25km away and there are some nice little single-track mountain roads that connect home to the pool. My wife is usually happy for me to throw on a rucksack and leave a couple of hours before her and meet the family at the pool, and that is a great way not to separate life and running too far.

Work takes me round the country, and if I can get in a run I usually will. They're usually shorter runs, and I might try and put some fartlek or speed work in on these days. If nothing else I get to explore new places, and that is good for the mind.

Events are really tricky to balance with family – especially straight line or loops. Where my wife (pre-kids) would be happy to try and snatch a view of me now and then, this really doesn't work with children. One method that does work is to be around for the start and about half an hour before the finish time, and the family heads off in between. But more normally, and especially on multi days, these events have to be 'just for me'.

I guess the best tip with all these things is to communicate. As runners we're used to managing ourselves, our thoughts and our needs. If I can tell the family what to expect, like when I'm doing my long run, then they know I'll come back a far nicer guy for having enjoyed my run. I had to grow some thick skin fast, when number two daughter started stringing sentences together with 'Daddy, you're stinky', but that has become a bit of game.

Accept you're single minded (you have to be), don't forget that rest time is an important part of training efficiently, and give that to the things that are important to you.

Steve Webb

The work–life balance is a funny one. My school always puts on parents' evenings or opens the door to Ofsted when in that crucial peak mileage week. This is what I think of work–life balance:

- Run and/or cycle to work. This is more possible than it sounds, and combining your commute and your daily dose of exercise can be an efficient way of saving time for family
- If your job lets you run during lunchtime, do it. Mine can't, so count yourself lucky and take the extra miles

- Ignore jealous colleagues who say, 'How come he has time to train for marathons?'. No point in persuading them how much sacrifice it takes. If anything, remind them that if you could train properly, you'd be faster
- You will miss lots of seemingly vital training due to work, especially when you end up working all weekend. Just remember to get out, even if it's a quick five-mile blast instead of a twenty. It will help you work better and keep you sane
- When you need to reschedule training due to work, be careful – over-upping the mileage to compensate can sometimes lead to further ruin

My wife tolerates this. She tolerates every sulk I have when a busy week at work decimates my training. She tolerates every torn calf muscle, and survived my year of plantar fasciitis. She has never advised me to miss a big race.

- Don't be like me and sulk when injured – see injury as a minor, character-building inconvenience and an opportunity to strengthen your core
- Your partner deserves a treat for tolerating your obsession with running. The night before my first marathon, I gave her a rather expensive dress. Do this, they deserve it, and the brownie points are priceless in value!
- Get them involved in your training – a couple of miles warm-down, a post-run walk in the countryside

Sal Chaffey

I'm forty-eight and did my first marathon thirty years ago. Then I followed the textbook advice of forty to fifty miles a week with a weekly three-hour run – very time-consuming! I now find that two runs each week are enough, and I'll enter a marathon and a fell race in the build-up to an ultra just to get that extra speed.

I'm a nurse married to a runner, and we have two girls who don't run but don't grumble too much about sitting in obscure lay-bys waiting to pour my coffee! We orienteer most weekends and the grandparents are quite used to us scheduling a visit to coincide with an event in a nearby forest or fell.

I train on my own as I'm very much a morning runner, but we are active members of our local orienteering club, putting on a couple of events each year and editing the newsletter. Someone once compared orienteering to playing chess while in oxygen debt because of the trade-off between fast running and complex navigation.

Running to or from work sometimes features in my training, and when the girls were small I had a sixteen-mile run I did in the 2½ hours when they were at playgroup. On one occasion I was behind schedule and got a lift for the last three miles! Naturally we were all-terrain buggy owners as well.

Phil Hodge

'How do you find time?' This is a question that is asked quite often, seemingly because it is presumed that to be an ultra runner, one cannot see any of the  family. As a father of three children under six, it is something I am constantly considering, how training can fit around family. I have looked at my own circumstances and tried to adapt my training to the opportunities I have, rather than getting frustrated at the lack of training time available. One approach has been to use training occasionally as commuting. I am fortunate that my wife can drop me off at work (in a school) two mornings a week when she doesn't work. This affords me the opportunity to run home over a hilly ten-mile road route. Equally a lift in from a colleague would achieve the same benefit.

My school is adjacent to a forest, so when classes finish, I can head out the door for anything from twenty minutes to an hour. The trails and hills there seem to have great benefit even when the days are short.

I take the school cross-country team – ironically, this has the benefit of slowing me down as there are plenty of new twelve-year-old runners (I do run with the fifteen to sixteen-year-olds occasionally, and this has the opposite benefit). These slow runs have had great benefit in forcing me to have easy 'easy' days – a maximum of thirty minutes and a gentle pace. This means that when I run on my own I can increase the pace and really attack the hills, knowing that I can have a gentle run

the next day with the pupils – it also means I can focus on the pupils and do not have to sacrifice a quality training day to help them.

Most important is the Saturday long run – three or so hours in the Mourne Mountains, Ireland, with three friends. We all got into ultras more or less at the same time, so they make for great training partners with similar goals in mind. Runs normally start at 8.00 or 8.30a.m. to limit time away from home, and the combination of hill, fell and trail has certainly had great benefits – something we notice when completing trail- or mountain-based ultras.

Annie Carrington

Getting the balance between work and life and running is a constant juggle, and after years of juggling I have managed to start to split my year into sections.

Being a self-employed gardener means that winter is my best time to get in solid training, and to build up my confidence to face the year's planned events. Three days' work maximum from December to April leaves time to attend to family needs, house stuff, and being at home when hungry teenagers appear from school. It also means that long training runs mid-week are possible, with friends and dogs; even mountain bike rides in wonderful frosty conditions. I have time to sit and study running plans and really look at what I can achieve, recce runs of planned races, discuss race instructions, and study maps. All day outings when everyone else is at work feel especially wonderful!

Then May to October descends – it feels like almost twenty-four-hour gardening, running has to become shorter distance and fit in definite slots, and a frenzy of juggling takes over. It is an immensely rewarding time but it can be manic, with bouts of completely overwhelming work. I have yet to find a way of managing these months in a way that keeps that work–life–running balance efficient and effective. But I am trying very hard to work it out … before I wear myself out.

Living with an Ultra Runner

Sue Carpenter-Parnell

If your other half is one of those crazy individuals who likes to push themselves to extremes and you want to be there for them along the way, maybe there are one or two things you might consider.

You could be in for nights spent at motels in the middle of nowhere, or even camping, in order to be near the race start. For some reason, we usually end up finding a Chinese restaurant for our pre-race meal, there always seems to be one in the one-horse towns throughout Canada. Cold early morning starts become the norm and you should be prepared to deal with blisters, cuts, grazes, upset stomachs and sunburn as the race progresses. Theirs, that is – not yours.

My husband has run several ultra races, including the Death Race, Sinister Seven and Lost Souls, covering various distances from 50km to 100 miles. I've supported him at all of these events and watched other partners do the same, to varying degrees. The hours can be long and boring, so always have books, magazines and so on to hand. If you can grab

some sleep, do so, but make sure you've packed an alarm clock!

The worst thing about being a supporter is the unknown. They may tell you they are due at the fifth aid station at 3a.m., you drive and park as near as possible, trek through the mud, carrying a fold-up chair, change of socks, running poles, extra water, and then wait. 3a.m. comes and goes and then you get a little concerned. At some races there's someone to check with to see if you've missed them because they went through earlier or they are taking longer than expected and haven't arrived. The worst thing is when nobody knows and it gets to 4a.m., still no sign, and someone runs into the aid station asking if anyone else saw the grizzly bear on the path.

To be honest, I can't say I enjoy being a supporter at these events, but I have nothing but admiration for runners who attempt these amazing feats. I'm really proud of my husband for pushing himself to the limit, achieving things that few others would even contemplate and setting an amazing example to our kids and grandkids.

So my final words of advice are: be organized, don't complain – your discomfort is nothing compared to theirs – and if you don't want to take on the responsibility of race support, ask someone else to do it. Accept that anything can happen, you can't always depend on time predictions – and last of all, have a cold beer waiting at the finish line!

Emily Webb

- It's very difficult if you don't have your own hobby as running takes over, so …
- Have your own hobby, preferably one that takes lots of time and commitment, so that you're not so secondary to the running (runners are a slave to the timetable)
- There's nothing worse than an injured runner, particularly having to listen to them. Pray that the injury goes away so that you can be left in peace!
- It's good for people who work hard in stressful jobs to have an outlet. Running is a good outlet
- Leave them to it

Sarah Hodge

- Make it clear from the start that you are not going to give any sympathy to running-related injuries or illnesses
- Be open to meeting fantastic, interesting people, who are a 'bit of craic!'
- I take great pleasure in seeing people's reactions when I explain that my husband runs ultra marathons
- Find out were the 'A' races are and begin to research the hotels, spas and shopping in the vicinity so that it becomes a holiday for you, too – and don't forget the babysitter!
- When your children are asked what they would like to do when they are older, take delight when they answer 'run up mountains'!

Aiden Hughes

NEEEEER! NEEEER! NEEER!

This must be the most annoying sound known to the husband of an ultra runner – the early morning, or as we booze hounds call it, the late night alarm. By the time she returns, the guilt settles in. She is invigorated, she has just pushed herself further than the day before, and she is ready to take on whatever the day has in store for her. My appreciation of her endeavours never really kicks in until she returns.

It was this focus and dedication that led me to her several years earlier. Having always been a jack-of-all-trades, it can sometimes be intimidating being married to a master of many. Tori has always been this way, whether it was globe trotting with her family, climbing the seven peaks, or beating the best swimmers that South-East Asia had to offer, she has always managed to negotiate her way to the top of the particular challenge laid out in front of her. Running was merely the next step on her remarkable self-fulfilling adventure that she calls life.

The biggest regret I have is that I never really felt a part of this. At first there is jealousy, then resentment, followed by a realization that in order to be at the top of your game, sacrifices have to be made. The fact that I feel as though I am one of them destroys me inside, yet how can I expect her to stop her achieving what most people only dream about? Anyway, off to work I go, and as usual I make a mental note to pick up some ear-plugs on my way home later …

CHAPTER 5

Getting to the Finish Line

The longer the race, the more you need the skills to harness your emotions and manage how you feel.

In the world of ultra distance, being in the right physical shape only gets you to the start line.

Getting to the finish line – having the race you want – requires you to do the following:

- **Use your head:** Make proactive and reactive choices that are consistent with your goals – and if it's a team event, the goals of the people around you – and with keeping you safe (self-reliance).
- **Manage your energy levels:** Feed your pace and pay attention to the Food-mood link: if in doubt, eat and drink – it will fix most things, particularly in blokes …
- **Harness your emotions:** All things being equal, *performance is emotional* and the difference on any given day will be how you choose to feel.
- **That's right:** before we can realistically entertain any goals around times and places we must first plan to finish. We've already seen that the DNF rates in the bigger races are significant, so a finish is special by any measure you care to use, simply because a significant proportion of the field will not get there. A reason that they won't is that they don't appreciate that performance is emotional.

April playground: late spring in Torridon, western Scotland.

Performance Is Emotional

Training is physical: racing, or performing, is emotional. It's about how you feel – how you manage and harness your emotions – or more specifically how you *choose* to feel. Which means that this is the only question in town:

How do I choose and plan to feel like I need to feel in order to have the race that I want?

Answer Number One: *Know what you are doing.*

Set Goals to Really Grab You

There are several neurological and physiological reasons why the discipline of goal-setting works, and in simple terms it is this: 'We generally get what we focus on.'

So set goals that help you focus on what you want – as opposed to what you don't want.

Goals Give Choices Meaning

Choices about 'What do I do now?' are meaningless without an objective to give context. In order to make correct choices which take you towards your goal you will need to have a goal or two in the first place …

Make it Matter

Your goals for the big stuff should grab you and shake you with excitement and nerves in equal measure – they should really matter, really mean something to you – they should come from the heart and they should move you. Only then is it time to add the SMART detail.

Make them Balance

In my experience, of those people who set goals – and, by the way, very few actually do, and even fewer will admit to it – most will set goals about what they want to achieve, targeting specific outcomes, such as being in the top ten, completing in ten hours.

Few will set goals relating to *how* they want to go about that, concentrating on the quality of the experience – for example 'With a smile for as long as I can; with head up and appreciating my surroundings; to be patient and trust my choices'.

Even fewer will set goals that do both: 'This is what I want, and this is how I want to do that' – for example 'I want to run tall, feel in control throughout, and to finish in the top half of the field'.

Use the Cues

Think of your how goals as your personal code of conduct for the race. They give you key words and phrases to focus on, such as 'Run tall … stay in control …'

You can use visualization to turn them into pictures, and you can choose music that makes you feel how you want to feel (for example, tall). Don't do the ipod thing? No worries, just sing to yourself – I do.

Answer Number Two: *Really know why you are doing it.*

'Self-motivation is everything.

When runners train for an event they want it.

When they begin an event they want it.

But at some point they stop wanting it.

And they quit.

Big events have a way of sifting out the talented runners, fit runners, fast runners.

The ones that remain? They are the ones who want it.

When the question "Why am I doing this?" arises time and again, they have the answer every single time.'

Andrew Thompson,
Appalachian Trail Record Holder

Putting It All Together

How will you know it's working? You will find yourself starting to experience the ultimate emotional state where you are doing what you want to do in the way you want to do it without actually being completely aware that it's happening. This is *flow* – otherwise known as *In The Zone*: and that, my friend, is mastery.

I Know This Because ...

In the summer of 2011 I attempted a double-header: two 100-mile mountain races within two months. In July that meant the Lakeland 100 in the UK, and in August, a mere four weeks later, it was the Ultra Tour Mont Blanc in France. To make it even more interesting, the week before UTMB I would be working as coach and guide to six runners who had come out to the French alps with **www.alpine-oasis. com** I squared that away by telling myself it would be good time on my feet in the mountains at a slower than normal pace.

I chose to make the Lakeland race a priority and I did indeed post a pb and my second second place. By contrast the wheels had started to come off at UTMB after 30km, and by the time I reached halfway at Courmayeur I was paying for not making it matter enough, as my diary of the race records:

'Bravo!' 'Courage!'

Late morning on Saturday, and the Italian ski town of Courmayeur looks every inch picture postcard under clear blue skies. I've just cleared the forest after a seriously long and steep zig-zag descent into what is the traditional halfway point of the race, and after what has been for me nearly twelve hours of physical and emotional ups and downs on a truly alpine scale.

We've also had every type of weather thrown at us during the previous 78km and some 4,400m of climbing and descending – but that's not the reason for my haunted expression: it's because I know that my race will stop right here. In fact I've known that for the last few hours, it's just that the Italians are not making it easy. Men, women, young and old are out on the race route shouting and clapping encouragement to the weary runners. It's the children – the bambinos – that get to me, 'doing' unbridled enthusiasm as only they know how. Thinking of my own boys just makes it worse, and I feel the tears start to bubble.

Then the UTMB race organization works a leverage trick of their own. Every runner has their full name and the flag of their country printed alongside their number, with the result that spectators can make it personal. So I have my name shouted by smiling faces as I close in on the municipal sports complex in the centre of town, which is the checkpoint. I feel a complete and utter fraud. My number is shouted ahead so that my dropbag containing spare kit can be found among the other 2,299 – and then the knife goes in, because I'm handed it by a smiling young Italian boy not much older than my eldest son: 'Bravo, Andy!'

I have to turn away as I'm in serious danger of bursting into tears right there, and walk the final few yards into the building trying desperately to smile and wave my thanks around a very wobbly bottom lip.

Up the stairs guided by kindly Italians and into what looks like a huge mess hall, where runners are seated setting new speed records in food consumption. I look for the chair furthest away from everyone and everything and make a beeline for it. As I sit down the dam bursts and the tears flow uninterrupted for what seems like many minutes.

Despite all my mental skills I can still see no way to do another 80km and 5,000m of climbing and descending. More importantly, I can't seem to make it matter enough, either. I'm now paying the price for skimping the mental and emotional prep and figuring I could complete this little jaunt on what pretty much amounts to momentum. Lakeland was always my priority – this (and the pre-race week) was an experiment. I was blasé, and now it's back to bite me.

It's taken twenty-five years of racing, but finally I have another first: Mouncey, Andy, UTMB 2011, Did Not Finish.

REVELATIONS FROM REAL RUNNERS

Getting to the Finish Line

John Oldroyd

The 100-mile event organized by the LDWA in 2010 was based in Dunkeld in Scotland, but was actually 105 miles. So when I reached the checkpoint at Aberfeldy, which was eighty-six miles from the start, there were still nineteen miles to the finish. But I didn't care. I'd had enough; I wasn't going to go another single mile. My feet were shredded. Now, that's not a figure of speech: it's an accurate description of the state of my feet. Walking on broken glass is a figure of speech, and that's also a pretty accurate description of what forward progress felt like. For the last few hours I had been in the dark zone feeling very sorry for myself. The damage had been done on a tarmac cycle path much earlier in the event, and my best efforts at taping had proved futile. You win some and you lose some, and I had completely lost it – well, certainly the skin from the soles of my feet. Beam me up, Scotty!

I told the checkpoint marshal that I was retiring, and offered my event tally. But he refused to accept it, with the words: 'I'm not going to let you retire.'

My brain had difficulty dealing with this. Was my English accent causing a communication problem? I pointed out the bloodstains that were now showing through on my trainers.

'Well, what do you expect; you've just done 86 miles!'

I tried appealing for pity: 'But it's so hard!'

'If it was easy, you wouldn't have bothered coming.'

Perhaps he could see that I was now about to burst into tears at this impasse. He offered to accept my tally and my retirement, but only after another half an hour. In the meantime I was led into the checkpoint and instructed to have a warm drink, something to eat, and new dressings on my feet. The checkpoint staff looked after my every need, and the first aid guy was great, though he did wince when he cut off the old dressing tape; the bowl of warm water where I placed my feet was bliss; and guess what? – I remembered that I had a clean pair of socks in my rucksack!

It was some time later that I thanked the checkpoint marshal and set off again towards the finish line. Very slowly, but I had lots to spare before the event cut-off times. That marshal's awareness of mood management was far better than mine, and I am grateful for his lesson in psychology.

So this is my tip for the future: managing your mood is the most important thing you have to do. Failure might be a possibility, but quitting is not an option. If you need to retire, well so be it; but you are only allowed to retire when you are not hungry and not thirsty. *Never, ever*, try to retire when you first reach a checkpoint: you must first eat, drink and tend to those contact points. You might then discover that your pain threshold is higher than you thought!

In Summary

- The longer the race, the more you need the skills to manage how you feel
- Getting to the finish line is less about the physical and more about the mental and emotional
- How can you ensure you feel how you need to feel in order to have the race you want?
- Set goals to really grab you
- Know what you are doing
- Make it matter, then make it SMART
- Make them balance – use process and outcome measures
- Know why you are doing it

CHAPTER 6

Are Your Feet Fit for Purpose?

Impact Assessment

Who doesn't want to flow across the landscape with hardly a footprint? Minimizing impact is the name of the game, and the consequences of mismanagement can lead to DNF. This is one of the areas of the sport where the *compound* and *cumulative* twins really come out to play. If you want to start to quantify the cumulative impact effect, then consider the following:

Speed dating for feet. Got any toes with nails still attached?

- Think about how many times your feet will strike the ground in a minute (an effective cadence is generally considered in many textbooks to be around 180 strides per minute on a flat road)
- Think about your typical mile pace
- Think about how many miles you will cover in an hour
- Think about how many hours you will be on your feet
- Consider the fact that each footfall will strike with around two to three times your bodyweight, depending on how fast you run

You can be as fit as a butcher's dog, have all the gear and the toys, and be motivated up to the eyeballs – but if your feet fail, it could be all over.

So ask yourself this: Do my footcare habits really prepare me for the challenge ahead?

Make Your Feet Your Friends

If I'm thinking clearly and managing my emotions, as long as my feet stay together I know I'll get to the finish.

And therein lies the rub: I've already argued that ultra running is a contact sport, and the ability to keep our points of contact intact is crucial in whether and how we get to the finish line. Described below are three key considerations that I think affect that outcome.

Regular Footcare Habits

As with any peak performance, a broad base provides a foundation for success, and bomb-proof race feet are made over time at home through care practices such as periodic checks with a chiropodist, how we cut our toenails, how we treat callousing, how much time we spend in/out of shoes, and what sort of shoe we spend most of our time in. The goal of regular footcare is to promote a structure fit for purpose: strong, shock-absorbing and flexible with a tough, flexible covering, and toenails optional – and that doesn't happen by chance.

Care of Callouses

The hard skin that builds up on certain areas of your foot is a natural response to reinforcing what the brain perceives as areas of weakness or pressure. Think of callouses as the body's sandbags – they are a good thing. However, a problem arises when they build up to such an extent that there is a huge difference between them and the adjoining skin. It is this area of contrast that is a potential problem for runners, as it is a site likely to blister – and getting a blister under a callous is no fun, either. Filing is the method typically used, and the objective of that regular care is to minimize the difference between the callouses and the normal skin so that the foot has as uniform and flexibly robust a covering as possible.

Prevention is better than cure – and far less painful.

Mid-Race Emergency Repairs

Assuming you pay attention to the warning sensations and take action before hotspots develop to full blisters, your journey is more likely to be a happy one for longer. The emphasis should be on prevention, so that means good habits pre-race, and the discipline during the race to take action in the early stages of a problem. That means stopping, identifying the cause, and then changing *something*.

Once you're at the blister stage, treatment is as follows:

- Clean the area
- Squeeze the blister to push the fluid to one raised side
- Pierce the blister through this side close to the healthy skin with a sterilized needle (available free and sealed from your GP)
- Waggle the needle to ensure the hole is larger than the needle so the hole does not seal up again
- Squeeze the fluid out of the hole and keep pushing until the blister is well and truly flat and all the fluid is expelled
- Pad the affected area with a cushioned absorbent patch such as moleskin

- Strap the patch securely with kinesiology tape*

* Also known as K-Tape: it moulds and sticks well, and unlike the second skin-type adhesive patches, it is very easy to remove

Blisters under Toenails

Blackened and bruised toenails are usually accompanied by a build-up of fluid under the nail and it will *hurt*. Treatment is about releasing the pressue under the nail, and that means removing the fluid: there will be screaming and crying and it will not be pretty, but it's got to be done. There are two ways to do this and you won't like either of them:

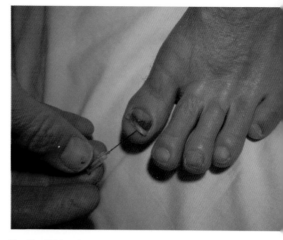

Treating blisters is not pretty ...

- **Horizonally:** Insert the needle between the nail and the nail bed, sliding the needle under the nail. Waggle, remove and squeeze down on the nail to expel the fluid in a high pressure squirt. Keep squeezing as much as you can handle.
- **Vertically:** Screw the needle down vertically through the top of the nail – and it is a screwdriver action. Keep going until you touch the bed. You will know when you do because it will *hurt*. Sorry. Squeeze the nail as above. This method is slower to heal, which means you will retain a hole for the fluid to escape for longer, and that's a *good* thing.

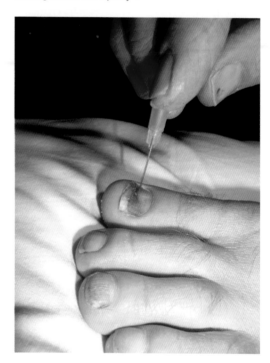

... and it hurts – but it works!

It's normal to leave the toenail operations until after the race, not least because it requires some fortitude and concentration. However, if you are in serious pain, then fixing it 'on the fly' may be the difference between a finish and a DNF. Be aware that not every member of a race medical team will know these techniques, so if you do choose to contract it out you might need to be prepared to add to their continuous professional development as well.

Foot repair kit: tick.

Blister Kit Contents
- Alcohol wipes
- Sterilized needles
- Moleskin padding, pre-cut
- Kinesiology tape
- Scissors
- Something to bite on (only kidding)

Footwear Choice

My preferences have been developed over the years: I like a roomy toebox, a reinforced plate under the forefoot, and protection offered by a high rand around the side. My sock of choice is the Injinji toe sock – though this combination will all change slightly for shorter ultras.

As shoe manufacturers continue to flood the market with more and more models and to retire others with increasing frequency, to my periodic frustration this is still a work in progress. Gone are the days when you could bank on a favourite shoe being around unchanged for a good few years. Today, even if the model persists it is likely be be 'improved' with a different material or what appears to be a small design tweak. Even this may change the fit, and that may mean you need to find another shoe.

Innovation has undoubted benefits and there are some wonderful pieces of footwear out there: the flip side is a bewildering choice as marketing gets more niche in an effort to make a shoe stand out from the crowd.

What follows is a checklist of recommended practice when choosing your footwear combination:

- **Experimentation:** The only way to be certain – and you may find you need different combinations for different distances and conditions.

- **Stockpile:** Once you find a make and a model you like, buy multiple pairs.

- **Local shop:** There's no substitue for the advice and service that comes from people who are passionate about what they do and want you to have the best running experience you can with the kit they offer. And then there's internet shopping where price often wins. My own position is that I try and split my purchasing between on-line and high street.

- **Gaiters:** Ankle gaiters can be a very useful addition in certain conditions. Be aware that even if the gaiters keep the bits out, if your shoe material is lightweight and porus then you may get small irritating bits passing directly into the shoe. Other common problems are that they ride up off the heel of the shoe and the undershoe strap wears through. Back to testing, I'm afraid …

- **Socks:** Single skin, padded, double skin, waterproof, anklet, mid-calf … the choices are many and varied and you just need to try them.

- **Toesocks:** I have long straight toes and in normal socks I used to suffer cut toes in long races where the nail of one pressed against the skin of another, regardless of how careful I was with cutting and smoothing the nail. Toesocks solved this at a stroke. The other thing I like is that they feel more secure – and that means less movement and that means less friction and likelihood of blisters. The flip side is that I know some runners who tend to run more on the forefoot and have found the snug sock fit actually reduced circulation to their feet.

- **Swelling feet:** Your feet will probably swell in the latter stages of a long race, which means the combination you start with may not be the one you need to finish with. Most events have a dropbag or crew facility, which means you can stash and collect some new kit along the route. Here are some of the things you can do:

  - Use an older shoe for the second half of the race
  - Use a shoe half a size larger
  - Use a different make and model for a different fit
  - Combine shoes from two different pairs if there is a stark difference left to right
  - Remove the footbed

- **Lacing:** The way the shoe is laced when you buy it may not be the way you need to have it to get the best fit for you. I know at least four combinations …

- **Boots:** Nothing in the rules says you can't wear boots. If you're mainly down to a walk and/or the underfoot conditions in winter are grim, then these may be the best choice. These days there are lots of lightweight boots to choose from, and even shoe-boot hybrids.

Barefoot Running: Barefaced Lie or..?

One of the big trends to hit the sport in the last few years has been the trend to minimalist footwear. A catalyst for that change in 2009 was Christopher McDougall's ground-breaking bestselling book *Born to Run*. Ever curious and still unconvinced I decided to conduct my own experiment to see what all the fuss was about:

- Could I reduce my footstrike impact and therefore delay the onset of muscle soreness?
- Could I become more mechanically efficient and effective?
- Could I make it just feel easier?

Taking my lead from the book I made these changes as part of my twelve-week preparation for the Lakeland 100-mile trail race in the summer of 2009:

- I chose three trigger words to focus on during my runs, which described how I wanted to feel: *smooth, light, easy*
- I included sections of barefoot walking and running into my training

- I added plyometric exercises – high intensity jumps, hops and suchlike – before and after some of my runs

On one level my experiment was a failure because I got the rate of progression wrong, completely overdid it, badly injured the muscles of both calves to the point of almost complete failure, and with three weeks to go I was out of the race. However, that is far from the full story:

- I know from my benchmark runs that I was in the shape of my life
- My stride pattern had changed: my stride length was shorter, I was off my heels more, my posture was more upright, and I felt more balanced
- I felt smoother and lighter over the rough stuff because I could change gear readily, and that meant I felt as if I held more momentum for longer

Since then I've built on these benefits and made these changes habitual – but you won't find me running around with a pair of gloves on my feet. I like some cushioning and protection – and I've also seen too many people wreck their feet to the point of Did Not Finish by choosing to use completely inappropriate minimal footwear *for them* at races. What this means is that I've taken the movement improvements from the barefoot principles into my normal trainers, and that means I think I get the best of both worlds.

The Barefoot Bottom Line

I believe the principles work and I have reaped some benefits. The flip side is the propensity for injury to the soft tissues of the lower leg, and there are now studies emerging that make that link – and of course there are also studies that don't. Once again the science is fledging, retrospective, and you will find the phrase 'it depends …' occurs quite a bit.

The challenge for runners wanting to experiment with this whole thing is to make the transition in a way and at a rate that you can handle – and in my experience that is a more measured approach and over a longer time than you might initially think. If it gives you the result you want in the way you want it, and you can make that stick over time – then in your world that's a result and *that's* all that matters.

Bombproof your Feet: How to get Started

Assess the Risk
- Start on grass which is fairly level going, dry, and free of glass, sharp stones, thorns, poo and so on
- If you don't know the ground, check it out first
- If you can get it, springy unspoiled moorland is a joy to run on barefoot
- Look for orthopaedic mattress-type quality in your great outdoors: it does exist! Cricket pitches and golf courses where public access exists are all good sites to start.

I Know This Because ...

Between 2008 and 2011 my summers revolved around being in shape to run the Lakeland 100, so the race has a particular significance for me. In 2012 two stats caught my attention. The first was that Terry Conway re-wrote the script on how to run and win over 100 miles in the Lake District. The other was that the race posted its lowest finishing rate ever: one out of every two people DNF. And this in an age when there are more navigational tools, more kit choice, better kit technology and training advice available then ever before.

Conditions were good – a bit soggy underfoot and a bit humid, but hey, it's the Lakes in summer (kind of) – and as the race has evolved since the first event in 2008, the route notes to runners and the race crew coverage and skill have all improved immeasurably. Kit technology and choice has changed radically, and then there are the shoes. Ah yes: shoes – or more accurately shoes and this whole 'minimalism' thing. I wrote this at the time:

Now I've read *Born To Run* and I'm a fan. I've also done my own experimenting with the barefoot principles, took it to the point of calf injury, figured some stuff out and made some adjustments to

my running style that have helped me. So for me it boils down to this: running 100 miles is a licence for repetitive strain injury writ large, and for your feet that's like someone taking a hammer to your delicate plates of meat repeatedly and with gusto for a whole day. And while I can support the whole 'being in touch with the Earth' thing, there's a world of difference between a symbiotic caress and a bone-crushing bearhug.

Since 2009 I've chosen a footwear combination which keeps my precious contact points comfortable, protected and reinforced for as much of 100 miles as possible. So while I lose toenails periodically – and that's excess weight and that's just fine because it's post-race – that's all I have to deal with. If my mind is sharp and I'm in control of my emotions I know my feet will get me to the finish line.

At some point someone will do a study on DNF numbers at L100, and I bet you there's a correlation with inappropriate/minimalist footwear.

Keep it Simple

You don't have to add another session to your training – you can simply whip your running shoes and socks off when you are out on a suitable trail and carry them in your hands while you get your feet out for a few strides.

A good way to start is to do this – terrain permitting – for the last part of your cool-down.

Relax and Enjoy the Ride

To really enjoy walking and running barefoot you will need to be able to relax all of you, and your feet in particular. This comes with confidence, and as you get used to the different sensations and are better able to read and anticipate the terrain. So you may start with fifty walking-jogging paces on a flat manicured lawn, and progress to barely in-control down-hills with big vocals – remember that as a kid?

How Much is Enough?

Well, remember that you are the expert on you, so the only way to truly know is to experiment with purpose and pay attention to the results you get.

- Not getting the results you want in the way you want them? Then change something!
- Are you so sore and tender afterwards that you can hardly walk? Then you've done too much, and maybe too fast
- Feet cut to ribbons and blistered? Too much and too rough, and again, maybe too fast
- Ankles really sore? Get on the flatter stuff first

A little soreness is OK; anything else is overkill.

A Final Word

You'll get some stares and you'll get some comments, because you see runners doing this all the time, right? Wrong.

Well, sometimes the key is to do what most people don't do.

You've chosen ultra-marathon running, which most people don't. So you're used to that. It helps define who you are, which makes *you* special.

In Summary

- Are your feet fit for purpose?
- It's about impact reduction and maintaining working integrity – so lighten up and keep it together
- Racing feet are made at home by regular footcare habits
- Running repairs: skills and discipline are required
- Prevention is best – act at the hotspot stage
- Getting to grips with blisters: what you need to know
- Help! Too many shoes to choose from! Narrowing your choices
- Getting to the bottom of barefoot running: believe the hype?
- Minimalism: the costs and benefits
- Bombproofing your feet: a beginner's guide

CHAPTER 7

Food and Fuel

'Eat food. Not too much. Mostly plants.'

Michael Pollan

There are whole books on the subject of food and fuel, and I'm not going to write another one here. If you're of the Twitter generation and are after something in less than 140 characters, then I think the one from Michael Pollan above is quite a good place to start.

I will give you some guidelines and principles as I see them, but beyond that you will have to experiment – again. That could be a long, periodically frustrating, though ultimately rewarding process, with a significant personal breakthrough that may well have benefits beyond your running performances.

It's entirely normal to be confused by the whole food-fuel-running thing. Nutritional advice from the great and good to society at large seems to change periodically, so why should ultra running be any different? Surely there are clues to be had from examining what the top boys and girls in the sport do – stands to reason they've figured out something that helps them be speedy, so there must be some consensus – right? Wrong.

Leading US ultra runner Dakota Jones illustrated the range of habits when he took a straw poll among some of the leading lights in the sport for www.irunfar.com in 2013:

'Geoff Roes ... once gave me a bacon sandwich and a donut on a run. He also claimed to have eaten 2,000 calories by 9a.m. that day. Anton Krupicka seems to subsist on Nutella and tortillas for 95 per cent of the time and stewed vegetables the rest. Anna Frost only ate grapes for a week and afterwards subsisted on crackers, tomatoes and mozzarella cheese. Brendan Trimboli took an even more extreme position on eating several years ago and just stopped doing it entirely. And that's just the start.'

Indeed it is. At the 2004 Western States 100-mile race in the USA, veteran Aussie Bill Thompson simply drove a truck through what conventional running-eating wisdom there was at the time. Eyebrows were raised and jaws dropped as part way through the race he was seen to work his way through champagne, steak and onions, and chocolate pudding and cream. Of course he went on to record a twenty-nine-hour finish. (*Ultrarunning* magazine December 2004).

The Future is Caveman?

So trend spotting seems a road to further confusion – but it's still happening. One of the biggest trends in the ultra-running fuel debate right now is the growing profile of fat and protein-led food regimes: the so-called 'caveman' or 'paleo diet', which is a world away from traditional carbohydrate-heavy habits popular in the Western world. As with any 'new' trend, the challenge is to separate the myths* from the truths, and to keep an eye on what the top boys and girls in the sport are doing. A key will be if it's still around in five to ten years' time, because at the moment although anecdotally there appears to be some very interesting and positive reactions emerging, science is still building a robust and comprehensive research-backed picture.

* Excellent further reading from *Human Evolution, Diet and Health* by Mark Hines

I Am My Research

As I write I am part way into my own experiment on this. After some thirty years in endurance sport in which I have never really looked at the 'calories in' part of the equation with any seriousness, at the end of 2013 I decided to do just that. My objective is to get most of my day-to-day dietary habits consistent with how I need my ultra-running engine to work during races. That is not happening at the moment because some of my day-to-day habits are at odds with how I (want to) race. This means educating my system so that most of my energy comes from my fat and protein stores, which are themselves part of a highly efficient reliable engine which can produce optimal performance over an extended period of time for very little effort.

Working with performance nutritionist Rebecca Dent (www.rebeccadent.co.uk), I made the first changes in November 2013, and while it's all still very much a work in progress, I've experienced some very interesting initial benefits, and it's safe to say that the more I've looked and experimented, the more curious I've become.

The following sections outline the properties that food as fuel should offer, and the relationship between food and performance output.

Fuel: Properties

What you ingest as fuel should do the following:

- Provide a steady flow of energy over a long period of time
- Provide an immediate 'pick-up' in an emergency
- Be palatable in a variety of weathers and temperatures
- Be portable
- Be easy to get at/into
- Cause minimal/no litter
- Be of low bulk/volume and high energy value
- Not cause bowel problems or nausea
- Make you smile and keep you moving

Finding Your Fuel of Choice

- Be prepared to experiment – it is the *only* way to really find what works for you

- Be prepared to feel sick, throw up, get constipated and have the trots as part of this learning. Sorry
- Be open-minded: I know runners who race on fast/junk food, and runners who have nothing except sport science concoctions, and both groups seem to get the results they want in the way they want
- Be prepared to go off plan: it is entirely normal mid-race to not fancy anything from your own supplies or to turn your nose up at the offering lovingly prepared by your support crew – but that ice cream being eaten by that little boy over there in the crowd looks just fine …
- Be prepared to need to eat and drink less in races over time as you become a more conditioned and confident ultra runner
- Be prepared to challenge some of the accepted advice out there – remember that the 'drink as much as you can' movement was driven, at least in part, by the vested interest that is the sports drink industry, and we now know that runners who drink in anticipation of their thirst will compromise their performance (see *Waterlogged* by Tim Noakes)

Simple

ULTRA FUEL

Task + Treats

Infrequent

Habits for High Performance: Lifestyle

- Eat less
- Eat to hunger
- Drink your water and watch your urine; clear is good, yellow and smelly is dehydrated
- Eat something of everything – how colourful is your meal?
- Eat for health first and fitness second
- Keep it real, affordable, easy and family friendly if you have one – remember if it's a faff …
- Check the cost benefits: you might get more performance gains for less effort/cost if you focused on one of the other fundamentals (like more running?)
- Keep it in perspective – we do this for free and it's supposed to be fun, remember?
- Have your own snack selection for travel/commute times

Habits for High Performance: Training

- Use fasting and depletion workouts
- Test as much as you can in training
- It's OK to get it wrong/feel awful in training

Nutrition → Health - Recovery + Fitness - Racing = Consistent Performance

Racing:
Task and Treats

In my running world food divides into two groups: food for task and food for treats. The former is quite simply fuel that provides a constant supply of energy over an extended period of time, and which we can harness for the task of relentless forward motion. The other one is the pick-up or shot in the arm that we use as a reward or a boost during a low point. (I used to love a jellybaby or two every time I turned a new page on the race route instructions.) Performance is indeed emotional, and making some of our food choices consistent with this principle is just another example of working in a way that is consistent with our psychology.

The following are helpful habits when you are wearing a number:

- Keep the calories coming in – a steady stream of savoury and sugar
- Drink to thirst
- Some salt may help, but again, the jury appears to be out on this one …
- Expect to eat/drink differently at different levels of intensity and in different environmental conditions – for example, you may need more in bad weather to keep moving, thinking *and* in order to generate enough heat
- Faff-free fuelling is essential and critical in bad weather when your focus narrows
- Eat on the climbs when you are walking
- Carry your own collapsible cup/flask
- Expect to lose weight and be OK. There's no evidence I can find that weight loss in excess of 2 per cent impairs performance, and figures of more than 10 per cent loss

are routinely recorded in ultra race top performers (T. Noakes, 2012).

Becoming More Fuel Efficient

Becoming a more economical runner – at least as far as your engine is concerned – can be a change that takes place without too much conscious thought and action. This is because:

- The more you run long, the more your body systems get used to operating on the move
- The easier it gets to operate on the move, the more confident you become
- The more confident you become, the more you start to explore and push – and part of *that* is lightening the load … you can go longer and easier and on less

This is, after all, the essence of the training effect:

> We get really good at what we do for most of the time.

Put simply, this means that all things being equal, we will get better at running long distances if we spend lots of time running long distances – and the even better news is that this will happen naturally because our brains are constantly looking for efficiency, effectiveness and the most energy-saving route to maximum performance. And *that's* because the primary function of the brain is to keep the organism safe – and *that* means always having a reserve to tap into for emergencies. (So if you've ever wondered why that runner who looks and moves like death can miraculously raise a sprint for the finish line, the answer at least in part lies with the primary function of our brain: always have something in your back pocket just in case …)

Confidence to lighten the load can result in two key changes the more you run ultras:

- You will, over time, carry and wear less gear during a race
- You will, over time, consume less food and drink during a race

While you can expect the latter to happen at least in part as part of a natural progression for the reasons described above, you can also give the process a push and actively condition yourself to become more camel-like in the quest for ultra-running fuel efficiency.

Fasting and Depletion Training

The process I am about to describe is based on my own experimentation. There is science to back it up, but to be perfectly honest the task of sifting it over, translating it into layman terms and marrying it with my own experience will have to wait for another book. I know what I've done and I know what has happened as a result, and I hope that's enough for most of you. For those of you who are curious about the science of the 'why', then studies by K. Baar (2013) and K. Praeyerik (2010) are referenced at the end of this book.

I was first introduced to this process in the 1990s by Steve Trew, my triathlon coach at the time. I was training for Ironman distance, and Steve had me doing my second session of the day at least four hours after my first. I was only allowed water and orange juice in that recovery window, which meant I went into that second session relatively depleted. Getting through it intact meant that my system had to source energy from my fat and protein stores instead, and become increasingly efficient at using the limited amount of sugar and carbohydrate fuel I was taking in during the first session. It was, unbeknown to me at the time, my first experience of fasting or *depletion* training, which might be described as follows:

To operate comfortably for increasing amounts of time on your feet while consuming progressively decreasing amounts of fuel and all the while continuing to think clearly: start with the end in mind.

To begin with it is advisable to start small at the start of the day. Therefore wake up, go run, then eat: like this you will be running in a depleted state for a relatively small amount of time, and have breakfast to look forward to – so it should be much easier to get your head around.

Getting Serious: A Guide for Making it Stick

- Give yourself a three to six-month window to make the change
- Choose one session on a regular basis where you practise making this change

- Take a full supply of fuel with you regardless of your consumption intention
- Keep it slow, and expect to get your pace/effort judgment wrong in the early stages: you may find that there is as much walking required as running, and what running there is, is at a slower pace than even your normal 'easy' pace
- It's OK to feel crap in the early stages
- Be strong! Even if you can only extend your envelope by fifteen minutes at a time you are still making progress: keep it really slow and be patient
- Start on flatter terrain
- Start at around two hours' duration, and build in increments from there
- Start with a full picnic of your usual foods, and progressively reduce the amount you eat and drink over the test period
- Eat and drink well post outing

Depletion Training: The Flip Side

Nausea and stomach problems as a result of your body struggling to digest and process fuel during a race can really ruin your ultra-running experience. So it also makes sense to practise running long and eating and drinking, because doing depletion to the neglect of all else will produce a very skewed system. It's also, I think, fundamentally unsafe and unhealthy. Remember that it is a process for a specific end – and there are other processes and other ends.

In Summary

- More experimentation, I'm afraid
- 'Caveman' diet: the initial indications are interesting
- Be clear what you need from your fuel
- Have food for task and food for treats
- How far do your daily habits support your competition aspirations?
- Practise habits for high performance lifestyle, training and racing
- You can train to be more fuel efficient by using fasting and depletion sessions

REVELATIONS FROM REAL RUNNERS

The Food Thing

Ken Letterie

We were stacking our poker chips and chowing down on calzones, Doritos and Lo Mein when the topic of the Arabian Homes Fun Run came up. It was a joke to most everyone in the room – 'fun' run? Just a few weeks earlier the Arabian Homes compound that we live in, had put on a fun run where participants did loops around the 1km compound perimeter (we had to stay inside the fifteen foot, razor wire-covered walls, of course). It is widely known to folks in the compound that I participate in crazy/insane running events that go for more than a marathon distance – and most everyone knows this not because they see me running, but rather because they see me *eat*.

John looks across the poker table at me and says, 'You have a very interesting running style.' He had been among the observers at the fun run. 'You don't seem to waste any energy – everything goes into forward motion. Even your head and shoulders stay at the same level the whole time – no bobbing up and down.'

I responded with an honest answer, 'I need to keep my head level so I can eat while running. It's tough to put down a hoagie or piece of pizza when your head is moving around.'

Well, this comment was met with a roomful of the most wholehearted laughter I've ever heard. Then it struck me that to almost anyone outside the ultra world, this was a comical explanation by someone who is notorious for destroying the buffet table, and had been given the childhood nickname of 'WhogMan'. To me it was something I had been training for.

There have been countless runs where I've fought with a Clif bar wrapper or argued with a Gu to just give up and let me win. Small lesson there, I now pre-tear my wrappers so they are easier to open on the run, and get the air out so they fit into the pocket of my handheld bag.

There have also been many instances where, following the annihilation of a buffet, I would go for a two-hour run, be it in the mountains near Pasadena, or on the treadmill in Arabian Homes. These 'buffet-busting' runs, as I call them, serve two purposes – they help speed the digestive process so I get a better night's sleep, as well as train me to run with an uncomfortable gut.

Well, all this training seemed to pay off at the 2012 Angeles Crest 100 race. It was a homecoming of sorts, where I would be back on the very trails around Mt Wilson that had got me into ultra running eighteen months earlier. At mile seventy-five, the notorious Chantry Flats aid station that sits at the base of Mt Wilson, I was warned by the medical crew that my 14lb weight loss was too high, and I should refuel before proceeding. I asked how many pounds I should try to get back before leaving the aid station, and they suggested six or seven. No worries, I thought, the next two hours will just be a buffet-busting run – and I proceeded to regain 9lb in twenty-five minutes.

It is on occasions like this that I am so thankful that I have found this wonderful sport of ultra running. It combines my truest passions in life – adventure, outdoors, personal challenges, and most of all – *food*.

Victoria Leckie

I'm lucky. I have an iron stomach. And wait for it … I don't 'do' race food!

We're bombarded with advice left, right and centre as to what to eat and what to drink. The running community is certainly a dogmatic one, but I think when something comes from years on the trails it may be a confidence to listen to others, but sometimes it is better to figure out your own strategy. Practise in training, listen to your body, and become as self-aware as you can so you can detect patterns in performance and the inevitable peaks and troughs as you experiment with different fuel.

As for me, my treats will commonly include Haribo gummies, nuts, raisins and cereal bars … more sweet than salty, but overall just a delectable array of the treats I'd normally opt for even when not out running. If you race in lots of different countries, another thing to consider is what's provided in races, from cheese and chocolate in France and more-ish malt loaf in the UK, to salty boiled potatoes in Nepal and cakes galore in South-East Asia: if you can handle these foods, why bother carrying your own supplies? Just make sure you enquire beforehand and plan ahead.

As for hydrating, work out what works for you. I'm often told off for not drinking enough, but I've learnt over the years that I simply don't need to drink as much. I used to try and force myself, but then after absorbing the words of Dr Tim Noakes in *Waterlogged*, I realized that the obsession to over-hydrate is one entirely fuelled (sorry!!) by the sports drinks industry, and many studies now confirm that we should just drink to our thirst.

Conclusion? Eat often, drink to thirst and listen to your body. To steal a line from Benjamin Spock: 'Trust yourself. You know more than you think you do.' Bon appétit!

Carolyn Hare

As I crouched down amongst the ferns at the command of my anguished gut, I vowed through gritted teeth that I would find a way to never, ever put myself through this again. 'This' being a 36.5-mile ultra run on the Spey-side Way, part of the Scottish Ultra-marathon Series.

It had all started swimmingly in an ankle-deep downpour, and was pleasant enough until mile eight, when my tried and tested nutrition system broke down into a groaning stomach and the inability to eat carb gels or solid food … by mile sixteen I was experiencing a food in/food out scenario and stopped eating altogether, slowed down, and just concentrated on taking in as many calories as possible via chocolate coconut milk and soya drinks. I slowly made it to the end as my stomach started to 'do a refuser' – yes, even drinking had become an issue. I completed the course in a little under 7½ hours – about an hour outside my original expectation.

The frustrating part of all this was that training, course recces and equipment couldn't have been better. Now if only I could control my guts! I had another crack at a shorter but hillier ultra three months later and seemed to have ironed out all these issues – but I had cheated and taken an Imodium that morning, so really I was back to the drawing board as far as nutrition went.

And so the experimentation began: non-wheat, non-dairy, home-made higher fat solid foods, carb gels were all out, and my trusty coconut water and drinks remained firmly on the menu. Which was great until the biggest caveat of all – moving to the Far East where none of the foods I had trialled and tested were readily available (but as you might expect, coconut water is widely drunk). Add this to the fact that my nutritional needs changed with the hotter, more humid climate, I was again back to the start, although with the same goal in mind: complete the Spey-side Way but in a more comfortable manner, with the focus on running rather than crouching!

The biggest lesson was to make sure there wasn't too much fluid in my stomach, so I first found out how much I sweated in an hour at a steady pace, and then made sure I didn't over-drink. CLIF bars eaten two mouthfuls at a time, crystallized ginger and salted prunes have been my most recent running fare, along with 50p piece-sized carob rice-balls – not something to be eaten on their own, but they do an excellent job of keeping the long runs comfortable. For now! The experimentation will continue, and what works may change between events. I go into this year's Ultra with my eyes wide open and my rucksack stocked with anything but carb gels.

Keep It Simple To Keep It Down

Talking with a former client of mine about gastronomic fun and games led us both to have a lightbulb moment or two. You see, it doesn't matter how swift and speedy you are, or how hard as nails … if you can't keep stuff down, then your career as an ultra runner will be short and messy. Endurance sport has many examples of athletes who excelled over the shorter distances, moved up, and then found they couldn't nail the fuel part. Game over.

Pete has been struggling with the stomach trouble since moving across to ultras from triathlon: nausea, throwing up, stomach cramps, you name it. Enjoy the journey? Not really. 'Be nice just to run with the insides staying inside, y'know?' After a couple of seasons of persevering through this he had collected a basket of experiences from which patterns and trends started to emerge. He started noticing a few things. Much of it appeared counter-intuitive and contrary to popular training advice he'd come across 'out there', so he started to check this by asking questions of folks he found himself running with – and me.

'Andy, I'm just partway through *Magic, Madness and Ultramarathon Running* and I'm amazed at how much food you can get down. I mean, Western States 100 – you're having a picnic! No way could I do that!'

'Well, I can do that if I'm chugging along, happy, in control and paying more attention to me than trying to race my ass off. If I'm really racing, on the red line, under stress, I struggle with the solid stuff and have to switch …. The other thing is at WS all that picnicking gave me the trots for the first thirty to forty miles.

You gotta remember that WS came quite early for me in ultra running, and I'm still trying to figure the basics and being influenced by what I read. So compared to what I do now I ate too much and some of it was the "wrong" stuff.'

My good friend Mike with whom I ran my first Fellsman (a sixty-two-mile jaunt across the Yorkshire Dales) in 2010 was also memorably pissed at the amount of cheese and jam sandwiches I could get down me when he was struggling to hold down just fluids. But I do like the simple basic solid foods – it's a comfort thing as well with me – I've just learned I need less food generally over the years. Part of that is conditioning – I'm just more economical generally – and part is confidence based on figuring out what works for me – and that's about paying attention to what happens when I'm out there.

'Do you use energy drinks?'

'Er, no – actually I don't. Well, I did in my tri days … but ultras? Now I come to think about it probably the last time I used them was my London-to-Dover run in 2003.'

'Hmm. You see, I've been using just energy drinks …'

'And look what's been happening. That's triathlon for you – everyone's on gels and energy drinks – the sport's awash with it. I was the same. And the marketing and training messages – many of those come from vested interests, remember. Three gels an hour? Printed on the side of the packet by the manufacturers. Fine if that works for you … but that's a lot of manufactured gook in a very short space of time …'

I remember listening to Marc Laithwaite (race director for Lakeland 100 – www.lakeland100.com) talking on the subject, and he was adamant that the less you put in and the simpler it is, the less there is to mess up the workings of the running machine. It's like if you're going to cycle round the world: you'd do it on a fully rigid, single speed mountain bike because there's less to go wrong, and if it does go wrong you can fix it easily.

Back to that conversation:

'So what do you use – just water?'

'Yeah. With or without gels, it varies – hot sweet tea if it's available – and a bit of salt as well.'

'What – capsules, tablets?'

'Well, I've used S-Caps in the past, but the last few years it's just been a small bag of table salt stashed where I can get it easily.'

'So just water and salt then?'

'Yeah, pretty much.'

'And how much water would you drink?'

'Ah! Probably way less than you think – certainly less than I did when I started. Depends on conditions, obviously, but to give you an idea, on Lakeland 100 I carry one 600ml bottle and it's rare I'll finish it between checkpoints.'

Pause.

'Looks like I'm switching to orange cordial and pork pies, then …'

Energy Depletion: The Consequences

All roads from a state of energy depletion can ultimately lead to a DNF, and even if this is not the primary cause, it is likely to be up there as a major contributing factor.

I Know This Because ...

I'm still on single-figure DNFs, which I figure isn't bad in thirty years racing. My two biggest were at UTMB 2011 and the 268-mile Spine Race in 2014. Both took place in big landscapes and both in bad weather. While I've already mentioned my UTMB in the context of 'Making It Matter', a contributing factor was that I also did not eat enough to stay warm and make good progress. This was also my undoing at the Spine Race

I eventually ground to a halt at 160 miles after three and a half days of English winter travel. I had been suffering from the effects of creeping hypothermia since the first day, which twice put me into a big hole. On reflection the lessons were these:

• I was probably too lean on the start line
• I did not eat enough carbohydrate
• I did not drink enough
• I was marginal with my clothing layers
• My ability to operate in a depleted state masked the early signs of trouble
• I was well prepared, highly motivated and it really did matter, and yet there still came a point where I could not fight the physiology

Physical
Slow down - *Cool down*
Disfunction - *Inefficient*
Damage - *Shutdown*   DNF

ENERGY DEPLETION CONSEQUENCES

Emotional
Mood management - *Decisions*
Irrationality - *Premature*   DNF

Mental
Decisions - *Pro/reactive*
Tactics - *Strategy*   DNF
Self Preservation - *Navigation*

Energy Depletion: Physical Consequences

Slow Down, Cool Down
When we slow down we cool down, and when we cool down we slow down some more, which means it's very easy to get into a downward spiral. Breaking out of that spiral is tough, and part of the reason for *that* is the associated degradation of our cognitive abilities – in other words, it gets harder to think straight and even register the decline as our focus narrows into survival mode. Those people with high levels of mental toughness can hang on in there for quite astonishing amounts of time, but ultimately the body will shut down unless this pattern is broken.

Arresting the decline takes decisive action

and high levels of motivation at a time when we'd really just like to sit down and have a hug and a nice cup of hot sweet tea. However, if we have clocked the warning signs, then decisive action should include some or all of the following: eat, drink, add clothes, and up the work rate. Give it time, but the good news is that it is entirely possible to recover and finish after such a collapse. Believe me, I know.

Disfunctional and Inefficient

If we continue to deteriorate, movement skills go to pot as we transition seemlessly from graceful gazelle to stomping, glowering ogre. Posture deteriorates, stride shortens, cadence and rhythm take a holiday, and suddenly we have the weight of the world on our shoulders drilling our feet into the ground. The increase in impact forces alone means that foot damage is more likely, and the quad muscles in the thighs – the biggest muscle in the body – take a disproportionate battering, which further degrades our ability to move fluidly. Somewhere down this line as the deterioration accelerates is a trip and a potentially catastrophic fall: game over.

The Ultra Runner Shuffle

We've all seen the ultra runner shuffle: it's not confined to the end of races, and it's not only in events beyond marathon distance, when the eyes become glassy, feet barely leave the ground, and posture almost doubles up. No wonder it's hard, because one of the consequences of the doubled-up posture is that it's a position of constriction and therefore really difficult to get air into the lungs, allowing the heart to pump the oxygenated blood around the body. Try breathing when you've got your head between your knees if you're still

not convinced. Our systems are designed to operate best in alignment, but while inefficient posture may be what we see or experience, it may still only be a symptom of the ultimate enemy: running out of juice.

Energy Depletion: Mental Consequences

Decision-making Fails

The deterioration in cognitive ability has already been mentioned, and one specific aspect of this that potentially speeds us towards DNF is the switch from proactivity to reactivity: we are no longer thinking ahead and planning a response – we are, at best, simply reacting to events within a bubble of interest that is steadily shrinking. If mental toughness is still the glue that is holding a rapidly deteriorating body together, then unless a stimulus is linked to the action of putting one foot in front of the other without falling over, it's likely that we just plain don't care.

Tactics and Strategy

At worse, these go completely out of the window. At best it's reduced to tactics in the *now* and those revolve exclusively around *Just. Getting. To. The. End/Checkpoint*. It's yet another symptom of a shrinking attention span where if it isn't essential, it isn't worth it.

Self-Preservation and Navigation

The simplest of navigational tasks can become a challenge of monstrous proportions when the tank is running dry. Add to this darkness, isolation and bad weather, and you are potentially into a life-threatening situation somewhere down the line. The upshot of this is that you are more likely to make mistakes, and that will mean you will be delayed or even lost, and this will be accompanied by an even more acute sense-of-humour failure. This in turn focuses your attention on the fact that you really now are in the s***as a result of your complete and utter failure to get the basics right. At this point your self-esteem curls up in a corner and throws in the towel.

Now you are firmly into a compound and cumulative downward spiral as more time out on the trail means more time for your physical condition and mindset to deteriorate – which in turn feeds your negative emotions – and those negative emotions then work through to poison your thoughts and your actions. You become locked into an emotional-mental-behavioural downward spiral, and the longer you're in, the harder it is to break out.

Your inability to see the big picture means you are likely to be spending time repeating the same behaviour that got you into this mess in the first place, in the vain hope that this will break the pattern. *And if you always do what you've always done …*

Once again it is possible to stage a rescue, but only if you fix the cause once you've done managing the symptoms – and because *performance is emotional*, this means changing how you feel *first*. The hard part is recognizing through the self-generated fog that you need to do something different to get to that point – and then being motivated enough to see that through.

Energy Depletion: Emotional Consequences

The emotional consequences of energy depletion can be summed up in two words: mood management. Moderation is one of the first casualties: you'll be all over the place and switching from deep despair to blissful happiness at the slightest stimulus. Small things become big things as your sense of proportionality takes a hit, and that means you start paying attention to things you shouldn't. This then feeds your decision making, which becomes irrational and premature, stimulating behaviour that is less than helpful at best, and guaranteed to further feed the downward spiral at worse.

Now that I've painted a truly black picture for you, the good news through all of this is that there are few things that eating and drinking won't fix – especially for blokes. If the wheels are coming off, then you can do far worse than having a default position as follows: *veered off track? Time for a snack …*

In Summary

- Energy depletion: the most common cause of racing under-performance?
- The consequences of energy depletion are physical, mental and emotional and occur in combinations
- Get your energy management right and you will be more than halfway home

CHAPTER 8

Training: How Far is Far Enough?

We have already seen that it's possible to compromise your race-day chances by running 'too long' in training – but that still begs the question 'How long is long enough?'. The answer inevitably starts with 'It depends …' but let's try to narrow that down somewhat anyway.

A typical benchmark that I've heard applied to endurance sport is that 'if you can do half the target distance comfortably... then you'll be able to manage the full effort'. Now that's OK except here's where we run into real life, because on this basis even a twenty-hour race means a ten-hour training outing – and for most of us with real jobs and families (and DIY) this isn't practical. A solution is to break this into two parts as a back-to-back outing mentioned earlier, but even before we get to the practical implications of trying to make this benchmark work, a common question I field is around the rate of progression towards a half race-day duration.

Here are some indicators to help you check your rate of build-up:

- How sore and tired you are the next day
- How even tempered – or not – you are: are you 'fun to be around'?
- How bright is your complexion – is your skin healthy?
- How your sleep patterns compare to normal
- How your heart rate compares to normal, when at rest and running

- How your perceived effort compares to normal – does climbing the stairs feel like climbing Everest?
- How productive and creative you are at work
- How much of a contribution you are making at home

Remember that running is supposed to add quality to our lives and to the people closest to us – and we do it by choice for the challenge, fun and pride. That's not to say we should be unbearably breezy all the time, but it does say something about watching the slide to our running becoming just another chore on the tick list.

So it may be that you are progressing at 10 per cent increase per week. And then again you may not. Maybe more. Maybe less. But if you are getting the results you want in the way that you want them – and you can make them stick over time – then guess what: it's a legitimate strategy for you regardless of what it says in the training manuals or what your best mate is doing.

Train Long to Race Long?

I remember first throwing this question around with a friend and coach of mine way back in the mid-2000s. We compared notes on our own experience and the people we had worked with and came up with the following list. Remember this was done way before I started looking for science to back up the trends I thought I was seeing as a coach and competitor – yet the reasons why (we think) people DNF at ultras makes for very familiar reading:

- Feet fall apart
- Loss of motivation
- Failure of fuelling strategy
- Timed out at checkpoints

There are others – yet we kept coming back to these four, and while this is a historical list and I've moved on in my understanding since then, you can see that some of the patterns we were observing some ten years ago have not changed much. Which begs this question: which of these factors is a function of 'not doing the distance' in training? Maybe some of the first, bits of the third, and perhaps the last – if failure to make a cut-off is not due to a navigation error.

Which begs another question: if it's rarely the distance on its own which stops people finishing, why do 'big' distances in training at all?

While we've seen earlier that there clearly *are* reasons for *not* doing big distances in training, there are also lots of reasons to do exactly the opposite. In general terms we are back to our 'confidence is the currency' principle, and underneath that there are also specific reasons

for positively choosing to spend extended 'time on feet' (TOF):

- Developing the body's ability to take in and use oxygen efficiently
- Developing the body's ability to become fuel efficient
- Testing shoe and sock combinations
- Toughening the feet
- Testing the other body-part contact areas (under arm, groin, and contact points with a bumbag or rucksack) prone to friction and chafing
- Testing fuelling strategies
- Learning how to manage mood
- Learning how to be self-sufficient
- Reducing the faff factor around personal kit and organization on the move

It's just that the distance makes bigger those factors that would otherwise be insignificant and/or that we would just put up with or get away with over shorter distances: therefore compound and cumulative at work once again:

Big distance = bigger cumulative effect … and bigger consequences if we get it wrong.

Far versus Fast

Before we get too carried away with this whole distance preoccupation, let's just pause and remember one thing that I think applies to us all, regardless of our ability:

The aim of (at least some of) the game is to get from the start to the finish line in the shortest possible time.

Group training: peer pressure in the search for speed.

Certainly the importance of this will vary hugely person to person, and for some races for some people the focus will be pretty much all about the journey – and yet, remember that one of the common features of an ultra-running race field is that the folks on the start line share a desire to be challenged. Whether that's being drawn to competition with others, or competition with themselves, is neither here nor there. What I think that all means is that however you cut it, there *is* a speed component to ultra running: thus to go faster we need to go faster.

These days at the top end of the sport if you aren't up to five-minute mile pace then you limit your chances even over distances of 100km – 100 miles, because if a break goes away on a runnable downhill part of the course even in the latter stages, then this is the speed it will probably happen at. Feats of the élite notwithstanding, a general principle more of us will be familiar with is that:

The faster we can cruise at, the easier the slower stuff feels.

And anyway, who doesn't like running fast(er)?

For those of you who are still wavering, here's a clincher: running fast is a very effective way to become more efficient, because to run fast(er) we have to move efficiently – otherwise we go slow. And efficiency is at the heart of ultra-running enjoyment and success. So whether your aspiration is a ten- or a five-minute mile, the principle applies: at some point your training should include some running that has you breathing harder than normal – and that's all good, because it will help you in the long run …

How Far is Far Enough: How to Figure it

We get really good at what we do most of. This is 'the training effect'. So it follows that to get really good at running we should run. Lots. At least as much as we can. Except we also know that as the distance increases, the less of a pure runner we need to be.

Exactly *how much* running is a right amount, and how far a longest run should be, seems to be a function of the following:

- What we want to do (the race, the goals)
- How much we want to do it (motivation)
- Where we are starting from (our background)
- What we can realistically commit to (how big a stretch it is)
- What we can practically do (the real life bit)
- How that will affect those closest to us (close personal relationships)
- How much those closest to us are prepared to support us (the buy-in bit)
- What we are prepared to give up (choices and sacrifices)
- What state – physically, mentally, emotionally – we are prepared to finish in, and how long we are prepared to spend recovering

Studies of top endurance athletes compiled by Tim Noakes in *The Lore of Running* (2001) led him to conclude that one of the key factors for success in running is indeed to do just that: run. Lots. Consistently.

For us mere mortals I think that translates into 'as often and as consistently as possible' given the factors above. What that actually means is that I don't know how far is far enough for your maximum training duration. It depends. I do think it's probably less than you think – and I do know this figure will probably change over time.

What I can say for certain is that there are huge benefits to *going long* in training – and there are also other ways in which we can prepare that will also get us across that finish line. The right combination for you? Is the right combination for you. And the best person to figure that out is you.

In Summary

- How far is far enough in training? It depends …
- Ultra running and real life: it needs to fit
- We do this for fun and it needs to enrich our lives and enhance our relationships
- Read the signals and build at a rate you can handle
- Going 'long' has benefits, and remember it's not about the distance per se
- Speed has a place and going 'fast(er)' in training has benefits for the long run
- There are benefits to 'going long' in training – and reasons why you should not
- How long do I need to go in training? Probably less than you think …

REVELATIONS FROM REAL RUNNERS

Too Much, Too Far, Too Soon

Sarah Ledbury

I fell into running, as so many women do, after having my second child, realizing I needed a cheap way to lose the pounds. I am lucky in that we live on the edge of the Peak District with plenty of off-road routes available straight out the door. It goes without saying that I was immediately hooked, and one thing led to another. Within twelve months I had joined a local running club and started to tackle longer races.

But it was too much, too soon, and inevitably injury followed in the form of achilles tendonitis and piriformis syndrome. I bought a road bike so I could keep up the fitness. Someone foolishly suggested a triathlon, but I couldn't swim. But I wasn't going to let that hold me back, so I took a couple of lessons and entered my first open water event.

I'm not sure when I started to feel unwell, it just sort of crept up on me over time.

I started to catch colds, then viruses, then everything else. As a teacher and Mum to two small children it was hard to avoid all those bugs. At first I thought I was overtraining so throttled back – though I didn't feel up to doing anything anyway, so it wasn't really a problem, but very little changed. I continued to struggle in and out of work, but to be quite honest it was a struggle to get out of bed most days, and a miracle if I got out of the door. My demeanour suffered, and unable to function as I wanted to, I became depressed.

I was tested for all sorts of things but nothing stood out. ME was banded about when everything was exhausted, and then we adopted the 'wait and see' approach. Not good. We sat at home and began to plan what we would do if/when I had to give up my job.

By May 2012 I was having difficulty digesting food and seemed to be plagued by gastrointestinal issues. It came to a head at the beginning of June, by which time I was referred to a gastroenterologist for a colonoscopy, which still drew a blank.

I started to adopt a bland diet called FODMAP, recommended by the specialist to help me recover and get me back on my feet. Remarkably, after a couple of weeks I started to feel great, *really* great. I started to think about exercise again, and got myself back into work on a regular basis. I was referred to an immunologist where food intolerances and allergies were investigated, and we began to compile a list of the foods that had been causing me problems … a slow job that still remains a work in progress. The theory is that I picked up 'something' whilst swimming outdoors, which led to my stomach lining becoming sensitive/intolerant to a wide range of foods. It may or may not improve as time unfolds, but as yet there has been little change and my diet remains severely restricted.

I ran purely for the love of it throughout last summer, sometimes short, sometimes long, but always with a big smile on my face! I had to be sensible and learn the lessons of 'too much, too soon', always with one eye on whether I was getting injured or what I was eating, but then trained hard through the winter, heading out in my balaclava and head torch most evenings after work, and for long runs on a weekend. I refused to be thwarted by the harsh weather and bought metal spikes for my feet!

Since the start of the 2013 I have not looked back. I am happy at home, succeeding at work, and am overjoyed to be running again. I am still being careful with training volume, and nutrition for the longer events is an art in itself (I must be the only mountain marathon competitor to take fresh eggs as a source of protein), but I continue to set PBs both in training and racing, and am injury free. Most importantly, I am healthy, enthusiastic and feel *great*!

If you are ever unsure of whether you can keep going, swallow hard, put your head down and keep going. Determination and a strong desire to succeed can overcome almost anything.

CHAPTER 9

Strength Training

I want to declare my position on this from the outset: I am an accredited strength-conditioning coach, I do curiosity quite well and I also run ultras. This means that I start from the position given to me by my professional training and personal experience: that *strength is good*.

For the last few years I've observed, read and experimented. What you don't have in this section are detailed conditioning plans you can just blindly follow – it isn't that simple, and you're not that simple either. What you *do* have is the result of all that experimentation as clear as I can make it, and a framework you can take to a conditioning specialist who can fill in the gaps for you.

Why Bother with Strength Training?

Strength training has two main advantages to the runner: first, it will help him get better at the chosen activity – so exercises are used which strengthen the prime working muscles employed during that activity; second, it will help prevent injury when doing that chosen activity – so exercises are used which strengthen the opposite muscles to those working during that activity in order to promote balance. Remember: you can't fire a cannon from a canoe … and all things being equal, 'the strong will survive (longer)'.

It's about *resilience*: as ultra runners we are required to operate in an upright position over an extended period of time on our feet at changing speeds over varied and challenging terrain, usually carrying something on our back; also to bounce back from a fall and then recover quickly so we can do it all again next week. Hands up if you can't see the strength requirement in that lot.

What Strength Training Won't Do

According to Laursen *et al* (2005), it won't improve your VO2 max or your lactate threshold – in other words how fast you can run, and how easy that feels the closer to your maximum you are. The good news is that for most of us ordinary mortals these are not limiting factors to a good ultra performance anyway, because we just don't get anywhere near those limits. (Remember at the start of this book I talked about having these tests done in 2012? Well I was embarrassed by how average my numbers were).

What Strength Training Will Do

Tidy You Up

Strength training will improve your mechanical running economy by holding everything firm and upright so you are not wasting energy trying to control a jelly-like torso. If you're upright, then your lungs will have more space to work in, and that's just going to make it all feel easier – never mind all the other benefits. Think 'cannon from a canoe', and remember the posture-backpack link.

Laursen's study reaches this conclusion, and my own experience also backs this up. The more energy you have to use for the moving forward bit, all things being equal the easier and faster you will be. Once again, you can probably get away with jelly characteristics over the shorter distances, but cumulatively over the big stuff..?

Power You Up

Strength and power training – the difference between the two terms is the *speed* with which you can move a load – will help you get up and down the hilly stuff. No doubt. There's a lot of research out there (I've listed some at the back of this book), and once again my own experience chimes in.

Lean and Mean

You will increase the proportion of your lean tissue – that's more muscles in your body. This is *not* the same as bulking up. You will lean down because muscles are fuel-hungry cells that need calories, and this means your metabolic rate will ramp up – in other words you will use more calories just to sit still. There is a point beyond which I think that becomes

a problem – ultras in extreme environments, for instance – and I still stand by the benefit: if you want to firm things up and lean them down, then the right strength training will do it for you.

Neglecting Strength

What's wrong with being strong? Nothing – except I see a lot of weak runners. Even without testing them I know they are weak because:

*   Their posture and running mechanics are awful, especially in the latter stages
*   They suffer from considerable muscle soreness
*   They are predisposed to soft tissue injuries
*   Recovery takes longer than it really should
*   They are single-speed and one direction
*   They are slow on big climbs and descents

Stop press: getting stronger is *at least* a significant ingredient in fixing all this.

Weak runners abound because most runners train by running because they like to run (M.D. Hoffman, E. Krishnan, 2013), and most ultra runners train by running more because they like to run even more than everyone else. And while Hoffman and Krishnan did find that among their study group the most popular 'other' activity was cycling, they also found that more than half the sample did not do consistent resistance training.

Other reasons/excuses I've come across for this strength neglect are:

*   I don't like it
*   I don't understand it

- I don't have a gym
- I don't want to bulk up
- I don't have the time
- I don't know what to do
- I don't know how to do it

Let's deal these excuses straightaway:

- **I don't like it:** In my experience this is a smokescreen for 'don't understand the value of it', or 'can't do it well/easily so feel like an idiot', or 'had a bad previous experience'. So it's not really about *like* per se.

- **I don't understand it:** Fair enough. While there is a ton of information available on strength training for sport, there is very little on strength training for ultra runners – and again, what there is, is hardly cast-iron conclusive. Good job you're reading this book, then.

- **I don't have a gym:** You don't need one. You might need some things that gyms are good for – like a coach or friends to work out with, or a reason to do it – but these things are not confined to an indoor facility.

- **I don't want to bulk up:** Have you ever tried bulking up? It's really hard work to achieve. Really! It's also perfectly possible to get super strong without the size: you just need to train for that outcome. (For example, the svelte former champion track cyclist Victoria Pendleton would in her prime be able to squat twice her bodyweight and then some. At least.)

No gym? No worries! All you need to get stronger are DIY sandbags, and a medicine ball.

- **I don't have the time:** Usually linked to 'I don't like it'. Well, you don't need to find the time for another forty-minute session – I'll show you the time-saving bit later – and the rest is just choices about how we do spend the time we have.

- **I don't know what to do:** Fair enough. Convinced of the value? Get curious or just keep reading.

- **I don't know how:** Learn how (and what) from an accredited strength coach.

Now this *just running* is all fine because it's perfectly possible to be weak and fast and still get the results you want – for a while and up to a point.

It's also perfectly natural to concentrate on the primary activity – the running – till you hit a plateau or something breaks, and *then* change your approach: doing something different and/or working with a coach, for example.

Strengthening Exercises

Core Conditioning

Core conditioning is not about doing a few planks or abdominal exercises – it's much more than that. It's about an ability to maintain a strong trunk – between hip and shoulder – while vertical, in motion and under pressure. That pressure can be physical (you are wearing a pack) and/or mental (you're in competition). So that's what you need to practise.

Lift Heavy

Learn how to lift effectively under accredited supervision. Specifically, learn how to perform what are called the Olympic lift exercises and their variations, for example squats, cleans, clean and jerks. These are all exercises that are performed in a standing position, use the whole body, and require thinking as well as doing.

Once you've mastered the technique, the fastest strength gains without bulking will come from using very heavy loads – near or at the maximum you can safely manage – for one, two or three repetitions at a time. It's not for the faint-hearted, but it works.

(*See also* 'Lift Heavy: Get Hungry' below.)

Move Explosively

Jump, hop and lunge-based exercises that are performed quickly and with high impact come under the term 'plyometrics.' I have found them to be an excellent way to improve running power and movement efficiency very quickly. I don't have any objective data, but I can tell you that I *feel* a very different runner when I've been doing my plyo for a while. Put simply, there's more balanced, flowing running and less plodding even over the long stuff – you might even say I'm faster.

The flip side is that these exercises are complex to master, and highly stressful on the soft tissues of the lower leg in particular. This means there's a high risk of injury. Getting the rate of progression right for you may be a process that takes many months. Once again, getting some qualified help in the early stages is an investment I recommend.

Ride a Bike

If you ride a bike regularly you may already have found that your running hill climbing is relatively strong. There is plenty of research linking the benefits of cycling to running per-formance, as cycling primarily uses the muscles of the upper leg and hip and these are also the main muscles used in run-walk climbing. If you want to use your cycling more specifically with your running in mind, here are three things to try – two of which can be used on or off road or on a turbo trainer or gym bike:

Pimp your strength training – add children!

- **Ride through treacle:** This exercise involves big gears and low pedal revolutions, and you should stay seated. Start at ninety pedal revolutions per minute for a few minutes at a time – count the number of times your left foot goes past the six o'clock position in thirty seconds – and over the weeks and months reduce this to around fifty. You should still be able to turn the gear even if the pedal speed is super slow. Stay still in the saddle and be aware that this type of riding places huge strain on the knees. Pain and discomfort here are signals you should heed – finding a rate of progression you can handle is key.

- **Standing power climbs:** This involves big gears and higher pedal revolutions, and you are out of the saddle breathing hard. If you want to get really specific you can match your pedal speed to your typical uphill running cadence.

- **Tow the baby:** One for new parents everywhere: your trailer bike is your friend! I could handle ours until the child was about three years old, but still recall a humbling emergency dismount on a local hill as Mouncey junior got progressively more of a dead weight. If you don't have a baby of your own I'm not recommending borrowing one either: get panniers and load them up.

Lift Heavy: Get Hungry

There is a key side effect from this type of training: you will want to eat more. This is because you are building more muscle, and muscles need fuel to operate. You are increasing your daily calorific requirement and probably raising your base metabolic rate in the process – in other words, how much energy you need to just 'tick over'. So I know what you're thinking: 'Hold all calls! I'll be down at the all-you-can-eat buffet!'

However, without wanting to pour cold water on this, I will give you a couple of things to think about, which for me are still a work in progress:

- **Muscle mass and running in extreme environments:** I think there's a question around at what point having a relatively high proportion of lean tissue becomes detrimental to running ultras in either hot or cold conditions, and that question for me is about the ability to manage body temperature.

- **Muscle mass and appetite:** I know from my own experiment so far that switching a diet from mainly carbohydrate- and sugar-based foods to more fat and protein smoothes out hunger pangs. In other words I am less hungry despite packing more lean tissue which needs more calories just to stand still. No, that doesn't make complete sense to me yet, either – but I'm working on it.

> ### I Know This Because ...
>
> A few years ago I decided to test the 'stretch – don't stretch' research. I stopped static stretching but retained some dynamic stretches as part of a running session, and some good habits post-running such as legs up, compression, contrast bathing. I was training hard and with focus and was getting into great shape. Unfortunately my lower leg muscles couldn't keep up as I took it to the point of injury. Once that was fixed I added lower leg stretches to the mix. Bingo. I now know I need to do some stretching – not every day and especially for my lower legs – and that I will pay for it if I don't.

Injury Prevention: Athlete First – Runner Second

Remember the training effect: *we get really good at what we spend most time doing.* So for us that means we get really good at running forwards in a straight line. Except trail ultras will have us up-down, sidestepping, leaping, jumping … and all over an extended period of time – and if our super-developed running muscles are working opposite limp-as-lettuce specimens, then it's a licence for injury at some point down the line.

Think about it this way: those big muscles at the front of the upper leg are the main ones we use for going uphill – but we need the guys at the back of the leg to do their job as well.

So to extend your running life you should do exercises and activities that have you moving in directions other than straight-line forward, also exercises that work the opposing muscles to the ones you mainly use when running, and activity that takes the weight off your feet.

Stretching

To stretch or not to stretch … the jury is still out. Some stiffness in the legs appears to be good for efficient running, and some flexibility in those muscles also appears to be part of an effective working formula. Where that balance is for you I couldn't tell you – but I know where it is for me.

Time-Saving Tips

Pre- and Post-Run Conditioning

Five to fifteen minutes before or after your run can work as well as, if not better than, forty minutes dedicated (gym) time. You need to be clear on your priorities – thus it is probably not helpful to lift heavy just before a key benchmark run, for instance – but if you are, then this is a real winner on the time management stakes.

You can work conditioning exercises into your daily training routine. Adopting wide to narrow arm positions makes the exercise progressively harder.

i-iii Walking lunges.

iv-ix Single leg squats.

x–xi Step-ups.

Do Your Homework

Look around your local area with new eyes:

- Where could you do your conditioning stuff?
- How could you use that playground?
- Is there a suitable log or rock you could use for lifting?

xii–xiv Step jumps.

It goes without saying that you always have a bag with your running stuff with you in your car, you have multiple ways of using your commute, and you always get your kit ready for the morning the night before. Right?

So too with your strength-training toys: the bike is always ready for instant departure, your heavy rucksack stands packed heavy, and your sandbags are stashed easy to reach in the shed.

xv–xvii Step hops.

Plyometric Practice

Add explosive jump-leap-hop movements into sections of your trail runs, and the more challenging the terrain, the better the playground: stream leaping, fast-feet drills through tree roots, rock-hopping and tree slalom are all great fun and games that also build your ability to really move.

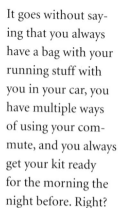

- **No gym? No worries:** There are a multitude of places and opportunities in your locality that can become your gym – you just need to look at your neighbourhood with new eyes. The local playground, train station, woods and anywhere with steps will get you started.

Using the local playground for pull-up plank exercises. This one is great for the postural muscles at the back of the shoulders.

- **Bags not bars:** You don't have to invest in a full weight-lifting home kit either. Sandbags will work just as well, and you can buy or make your own and fill to suit.

- **Boys not bags:** Small children can also be employed as lifting loads. I understand girls are also available though I have no direct experience of that being a father of two boys.

- **Get loaded:** Power hiking – that's fast walking – with a very heavy rucksack is great conditioning for the torso and lower body, and when you are able to handle the challenge of the load on steep/uneven terrain you can up the workrate to get a serious heart-and-lungs workout as well.

The challenge is to do all of this while maintaining good posture.

Using boots is to be recommended, and trekking poles can add another dimension as well.

This is one of the most high intensity, highly effective strength and power workouts I know for folks who want to move well through the hills – and not a gym in sight.

In Summary

- Ultra running is a strength sport – resilience is required
- Check the demands/requirements of your sport: how conditioned are you?
- Conditioning to get better and conditioning to stay healthy
- Most runners train by running – and are weak
- There are reasons or excuses for this – take your pick
- You can be weak and fast – for a while
- Core conditioning means torso strength
- Lift heavy, get hungry
- Move explosively
- Ride a bike
- Learn to hike under load
- No gym? No worries!
- No time? No worries either

CHAPTER 10

Night Running: Tips and Torches

Running solo with confidence through the night is a special part of an ultra-marathon running experience. Many of the big races will require you to start or finish in darkness and/or run through the night, but even if your race plans don't cross into this territory, adding a dark dimension to your running will open up a whole new world. It's a skill–confidence–kit combination, and this section gives you some tips to shed light on the subject.

Night time is the right time – although the skill set is slightly different.

- **Simple to start:** Start on familiar territory with friends in good weather where the underfoot conditions are easy and you can still find your way with a good light. Full moon nights under clear skies make it magical and can be almost torch free.

- **Slow is fine:** It's normal to be slower at night, so gear up, relax, and enjoy the experience at a pace you are comfortable with. (A notable exception to this is that if you are racing through the night after a scorcher of a day, then this cooler period might just be the best time to don your personal searchlight and put the hammer down ...)

- **Get a good light:** Minimalist is fine, but first and foremost you want to see where you are going. Power output is measured in lumens, and 200 of these beauties will give you your very own personal searchlight. However, most people on most courses/outings will find a unit with half this rating number perfectly adequate. A diffuse beam option will give you a broad light, which can be easier to run under than a bright, narrow focus beam. Any other gizmos and features are personal choice and dictated by how much you want to spend – just test it for 'faff factor' and discard it if it scores. Your choice should be simple, easy and comfortable to use, and do the job – and with torch technology these days you can get great kit for increasingly less money.

Experienced mountain racers will tell you that it's good practice to have a primary light, a secondary one, and spare batteries – with the secondary one easy to access when your primary fails and your world turns black. Lithium batteries tend to last longer, cold weather will drain all battery life faster, and you should wear your light *under a hood* if the weather is bad.

A recent innovation is variable or reactive light technology – the torch automatically adjusts the power it puts out according to need, which is calculated through a sensor. This means that typically the unit will dim for close-up work such as reading a map. This makes reading much easier, as the detail is not bleached out by bright light at close quarters.

- **Making the transition:** Dusk can be the trickiest time. As the light fades your eyes are making continual adjustments, and your depth perception in particular will vary. This is a time to slow down, relax, and allow body and mind to make the adjustments in time with the changing conditions.

- **'Remember the view' rule:** Stop – look at the view – then start running again. Attempting both simultaneously just results in stubbed toes at best, and we all know what that leads to …

CHAPTER 11

Innovations in Ultra Running

The sport of ultra running has exploded over the last few years, with more coverage, more races, more people running, more opinions and more new stuff to play with. For what is a fundamentally simple sport requiring not much more than shorts and trainers it's amazing how easy it's been to make it complicated and expensive.

Need convincing? Next time you're on a start line have a look at the folks around you and tot up the value of what they are wearing and carrying. Then remember that here in our small island, England is still quite repressed on the Gucci gear front – but go ultra running in Europe and you will experience a whole new level of personal wardrobe.

There's no doubt that there have been some wonderful kit innovations that are a joy to use and wear – fabric and head torch technology, for example, are unrecognizable from ten years ago. For me there are three changes of note:

- Minimalist footwear (already mentioned)
- Trekking poles
- Compression clothing

Trekking poles can easily become a hindrance unless you take time to learn to use them effectively.

Pole tips close to the ankles, wrist loop, head up.

Opposite arm with the opposite leg, elbows in, upright posture.

Recovering the pole with a relaxed grip.

What are the Top Runners Using?

Kit endorsements and sponsor commitments notwithstanding, the top boys and girls will only be doing or using stuff that helps them go faster more consistently. So a quick clue is to have a look at the front end of the field. Taking the top races around the world, and in my opinion trekking poles seem to be used by about half of the leading runners. This is skewed on continental Europe where poles are part of the outdoor culture, and in the US where they are definitely not.

The picture is also skewed as regards compression clothing: in Asia and on the continent it seems very much part of the uniform, whereas here and in the US the pattern is less clear. All of which means that for me, the jury is still out – even though my personal experience with both innovations has been that there are benefits to be had. To paraphrase something someone once said: 'If you think it does or you think it doesn't, you're probably right.'

What does the Science Say?

The problem with innovations is that they are new, and that means two things: someone, somewhere has a vested interest in selling the perceived benefits, and because they are new they can't pass the test of time. Compression clothing has been used for years by the medical profession to manage symptoms of poor leg circulation and conditions such as deep vein thrombosis. So there is some robust science behind it. The sport application is more recent, and while there is some science, it's still at the fledgling stage and the good studies recognize this. It's a similar situation with poles: there is stuff out there looking at hiking, but a specific ultra-running application I've yet to find.

Five to Ten Years on: How Mainstream Is It?

If it's still around and more mainstream in a few years' time, then the chances are that there really is something to it: it solves a problem, and is easy to use, scientifically solid, and pitched at a right price. Unfortunately time travel is still a work in progress, which means we'll all just have to wait and see.

Epilogue

Is It Journey or Destination?

'Andy, we wrote "Don't give up" and you gave up.'

Cracking The Spine exposed my race decisions to a level of public scrutiny I've never previously known. After my Did Not Finish – also known as Did Nothing Fatal – at the Spine Race in January 2014, I did the rounds of the thirteen participating schools where the pupils had followed the race live on-line as they were clocking their own miles as part of the running challenge I'd set them. They all knew I'd binned it after 160 of the 268 winter miles on the Pennine Way, and they were full of questions. Some were pure comedy:

'Do you need a beard to keep your chin warm?'

'What if you're on a mountain and need a Number Two?'

'Why not attach a rocket pack?'

Some were clever:

'Why didn't you stop at the pubs?'

'Why did they have the race in winter?'

'How long would it have taken to get to the finish by car?'

And some were just too close for comfort:

'Did you enjoy the race until you stopped?'

'What did you feel like when you had to stop?'

'… and why did you stop, anyway?'

The prize for the killer question went to a young man at Cowling primary school near Keighley, who had cunningly swapped a question mark for a full stop, thereby presenting me with a statement that stopped me dead. Cowling school has eight steps for success, and one of those is indeed *Don't Give Up*. I, on the other hand, had clearly not done my homework …

The only answers that wash with a young and extremely discerning audience are those that come from the heart. I knew this anyway, but this project had taken that understanding to a new level and tested my authenticity as never before. The scrutiny had also caused me to start to question my decision to stop before the finish line:

- Was it really good mountain-sense?
- Was there really any way I could have come back from that point?
- Did I really truly give it my all?

Absolutely pointless. The more time passes, the more blurred the context of that decision on 14 January 2014 becomes. It is time, place and situation specific – and I believed it was the best decision I could make at the time, given the nature of the challenge ahead and the resources at my disposal. Except I wanted to check it – because the kids demand and deserve it.

Words of Wisdom

A couple of days after my withdrawal from the race I was sitting with my eldest son Tom at home. There was a pause in the conversation, and then he looked at me with all the wisdom and utter certainty of his six years:

'Dad,' he said, 'It doesn't matter that you didn't reach the finish – as long as you tried your best.'

Oh. My. Word. I didn't trust myself to reply for a good few seconds, and when I did I suspect it wasn't the most articulate or insightful sentence I've ever strung together.

The truth was, of course, that it did matter to reach the finish line – it's just that it mattered more to do my best in the face of a challenge that was new, big and scary on many levels. On that occasion my best wasn't quite good enough, but lots of things did go well – and *that* delighted me – and I'll use those as a springboard for the next time.

The schools, while giving me a sympathetic hug in public, were also quietly delighted I had failed: 'Great!' they said. 'We can get so much more learning out of this for the pupils':

Success at something worthwhile isn't easy, it doesn't happen in a straight line, and it isn't something someone else gives you.

Yet, as long as you practise the skills of perseverance and learning, you will get there. And when you do you will find that the finish line will become a start line for something else. That could be another race or it could be another direction entirely. Whatever it is, you will face it with a little more steel and more smiles than you might have done previously. Running an ultra can do that to you.

Andy Mouncey, 2014

Index